A BEGINNER'S GUIDE TO ZEN AND THE ART OF
SNOWBOARDING
A COMPLETE STEP-BY-STEP GUIDE

W9-CGV-252

A BEGINNER'S GUIDE TO ZEN AND THE ART OF
SNOWBOARDING

A COMPLETE STEP-BY-STEP GUIDE

**WRITTEN & ILLUSTRATED BY ELENA GARCIA
WITH TECHNICAL ASSISTANCE
FROM KERRI HANNON**

THANKS:
To the instructors at Breckenridge who helped me edit this book and bolstered me with endless encouragement. And to all those wonderful and zany folks like Todd, Jody, John, Joe, and Brad for being there, sharing their knowledge, laughing with me, and sharing the fun.

Library of Congress Catalog Card No. 89–083944

First Edition, October 1990

ISBN: 0–934965–05–6

AMBERCO PRESS
Berkeley, CA
10 9 8 7 6 5 4 3 2 1

Composition: Another Point, Inc.

Copyright © 1990 by Elena Garcia. All rights reserved, including reproduction in any form, in whole or in part, without written permission from the copyright holder except for short excerpts for purposes of review.

SPECIAL THANKS:
To my friends, who got me involved in winter sports, the Applegarth family, who took me on my first ski trip, and my good friend and comrade in sports, Wendy. Thanks to Ralph, who taught me how to work, and Winston, a friend who spent thirteen years making me into a skier and then shared the lumps and bumps of learning to snowboard with me. And finally, thanks to Margie and Sylvia, who made sure I was fed, partied and exercised occasionally during the final phases of writing this book. Thank you all for your support, encouragement and suggestions.

A VERY SPECIAL THANKS:
To Kerri Hannon, who was instrumental in producing this book. Not only is she a top professional snowboarder and a wealth of information, but a pleasure to work with, whether on the hill or at the computer. Her enthusiasm for the sport is contagious. I hope you catch it!

DEDICATED TO:
All of you who have said "It looks like fun! Let's try it!" You have survived ice-covered roads, sub-Arctic temperatures, that day you were hating life (remember your first lesson?), countless questions from curious skiers and onlookers and serious scrutiny from resort management. You are the ambassadors of a winter sport that has taken the mountains by storm around the world. May you always have sunny powder days and perfect turns.

CONTENTS:

NOTES ON THE FIRST EDITION:

When I wanted to learn how to snow-board, I looked for a book, to no avail. My running buddy and first snowboarding friend Wendy came up with the idea of writing a book on the subject. The idea seemed farfetched at the time, but as Wendy, Winston and I struggled through those first few days of endlessly repeating the same mistakes while we were trying to find our edges, the idea seemed to gain merit and substance.

Enclosed in these pages is the end product of those first ideas. I hope it will keep you from repeating our mistakes, or at least keep you from repeating them so many times! Fun, safe riding is what we're all after, not lumps and bumps.

I look forward to hearing from you, from the beginning to intermediate snowboard rider, on what you think of this book and how and where you think it could be improved. Please write me % AMBERCO Press, P.O. Box 5038, Berkeley, CA 94705.

Elena Garcia, April 1990

PREFACE: USING THIS BOOK:

If you have never skied or snowboarded before, you should read this book in the order I've written it without skipping around. This is because I've written the terms, theories and maneuvers in the order you probably ought to learn them. Often I'll use a term or theory that I've explained in one section to explain a term, theory or maneuver in a subsequent section. If you just skip to the latter section without reading the first one, chances are you'll be lost.

But I know there are those of you who will want to read "Killer Rides on Thunder Mountain" (yow!) before you read "The Basic Theory of Turning the Snowboard" (yawn!). For this reason I've included a glossary of terms at the back of the book. That way, if you read, for instance, the term "face plant" without having read through the section about how to do one (and, more importantly, how to avoid doing one!), you'll be able to look it up and get an idea of what we're discussing.

It's important for you to get a good, basic theoretical understanding of how things work, and to step through the humiliating beginner's maneuvers before you get out on the hill and attempt your first ride. I know snowboarding looks easy when you see that professional rider swooping down the hill. But you have to start at the beginning, just like everyone else. Trying to rush the process will only result in frustration, embarrassment and possibly injury (to you or someone you collide with).

Take it easy, and have fun!

FIG. 1: USING THIS BOOK

Zen and the Art of Snowboarding

CHAPTER ONE: INTRODUCTION

HI! I'M YOUR INSTRUCTOR. FOLLOW ME INTO THE WILD WORLD OF SNOWBOARDING!

A SHORT HISTORY OF SNOWBOARDING:

Back in the 1960's, when the skiing crowd was worrying about what wax to use and whether or not knickers should be the latest rage, some backwoods pioneers were giving birth to the exciting winter sport now known as snowboarding. Invented by marrying the sports of skiing, skateboarding and surfing, snowboarding beginnings were rather inauspicious.

The first snowboards were so primitive by today's standards they hardly resembled modern boards at all. They were crudely made and slow with few or none of the design and construction characteristics that could afford the rider much control over where the board was going or how fast it got there. Bindings were nonexistent. The flexibility and profile of the board were not yet perfected, so steering was difficult if not impossible. As a result, in those early days, aficionados of the sport measured the success of a particular ride not by grace or control, but by speed and duration. Anything over ten

seconds was considered a good ride. Scary, but good.

Brunswick Corporation was one of the first large commercial concerns to seize on the then-infant sport of snowboarding. They produced a board designed by Sherwin Poppin called the "Snurfer." It resembled a ridiculously large skateboard with an upturned nose, but with no wheels. For traction there were steel tacks driven up through the bottom of the board so that the rider could stand on the protruding points. A rope attached to the nose of the board and held by the rider barely afforded a hint of directional control. So, to the amazement of onlookers, early riders, obviously possessing either nerves of steel, brains of sawdust or a combination of the two, would get a running start, fling down an awkward-looking device that resembled an Egyptian bed of nails, willingly jump aboard and fight for control until either reaching the bottom of the hill or performing a spectacular crowd-pleasing wipeout. Still, anything over ten seconds was considered a good ride. Scary, but good.

But the early pioneers weren't satisfied to let the "crash-and-burn" approach represent the pinnacle of their success. Instead, they were continually experimenting with new design and construction techniques, always trying to produce boards that were both faster and easier to control. Tom Sims, later to become a giant in the field, was among the first to build and test boards constructed with fiberglass and wood composites, P-tex bases and steel edges. Demetre Malovich, inventor and manufacturer of the successful "Winterstick" board, introduced sidecut, sandwich construction and swallowtails to his board designs. Jake Burton Carpenter revolutionized snowboarding by introducing bindings to the sport.

The ideas, concepts and techniques developed by these and other snowboarding pioneers quickly found their way into the commercial arena of a burgeoning snowboarding industry. Here their advances were combined with the technologies available to modern ski manufacturers to produce ever more sophisticated, high-performance boards.

But it wasn't only technical success that has made snowboarding the widely enjoyed sport it is today. All the experimentation and advances had to be supported by a group of devotees. To attract the public to the sport, manufacturers did what they often do to gain a higher profile: They held races! From the beginning, watching snowboarders race

caught the interest, if not the imagination, of the winter sporting public. The National Snurfing Championships, held in 1980 with a purse of $250, was the first organized snowboarding race held on a national scale. Soon after, the world championships were held at Soda Springs resort in California. In 1986, Breckenridge, Colorado, opened its doors to snowboarding by hosting its version of the world championships.

With the high-profile nature of the competitions, more and more people were exposed to and eventually tried snowboarding. Just as importantly, ski resort managements, which had previously often seen snowboarding as an aberration, slowly began allowing snowboarding in more and more areas.

Today, snowboarding is widely accepted and its equipment is as high-tech as the latest skiing gear, with advances appearing every season. And this owes thanks to the tenacity and inventiveness of multitudes of snowboard enthusiasts. They invented, tested, reinvented and retested the equipment, often paying for progress with sore necks and bruised butts. They have campaigned, cajoled, pleaded and argued with resort management to allow snowboarding on resort slopes. They have made the learning of this sport easier because of special-

FIG. 2: SNOWBOARDING PIONEER

ized equipment and instruction. They have cleared the path, and now it's your turn!

ZEN AND THE ART OF SNOWBOARDING:

Learning the basic skills and maneuvers of any sport are your building blocks to getting really good. In learning to snowboard, a solid foundation of these early skills and maneuvers will lead you into a world of exhilarating downhill rides and the breathtaking winter wonderland unique to the high country.

You want the basic skills and maneuvers to become easy, natural movements. This is most quickly achieved if you have a solid understanding of these maneuvers, are able to observe an experienced rider and can spend several consecutive days in practicing on the slopes. Your progress will be apparent each day, and you will spend less time making the same mistakes.

An important aspect of learning is the technique of visualization. As you read through the maneuvers in this book, close your eyes and imagine exactly what it's like to do them. Then physically step through the motions as you visualize the maneuver. It's even better if you do it with your gear on. For this, the living room rug or kitchen floor is a great place to start. (Put some duct tape over your edges before you start cutting the rug or scratching the floor!) Get familiar with your equipment. Pull on those boots, strap on that board. Feel the flex. Remember that you will eventually want your snowboard to become an extension of you. Imagine yourself elegantly carving turns, gracefully winding your way down the slope.

Be forewarned that it's not that easy once you get out on the hill. You'll need lots of patience and perseverance for learning! You're going to feel awkward

FIG. 3: VISUALIZE BEFORE YOU GO!

and fall a lot at first, but frustration and anger at your mistakes won't make it any better, and impatience will just slow the learning process. By all means, take lessons if they are available in your area; they will help you to learn faster. In the event lessons are not available, be as informed as you can. And practice!

When you're feeling awkward, stupid, frustrated and cold, take a moment to remember that we're all out here to have fun. Learn to laugh at your mistakes! Spare the unsuspecting skier who asks, "Is it any fun?" just after your fifteenth face plant. They don't deserve a verbal attack. Your frustration isn't their fault. Be courteous and answer the same questions you asked not long ago.

WHAT TO EXPECT:

The whole idea of this book, of course, is to try to let you know what to expect and how to deal with it once you start snowboarding. Much of my advice is very specific— how to mount a chairlift or perform a particular type of turn. Other advice is more general. But just because it's general in nature doesn't mean it's any less important! Following are a few general things you should know about snowboarding before you get out on the slopes.

FIG. 4: A TYPICAL NON-ZEN ATTITUDE

First, snowboarding is a very athletic sport, one which you will be learning at a high altitude. Being in good shape to begin with will help you during the learning stages. If you're not in shape, get moving before you go snowboarding! Biking, swimming and running are all excellent conditioning exercises.

Another thing you have to realize is that you will fall a lot in the beginning. Even if you're the ace-number-one, all-out, super-cool athlete, you're going to fall. You will get cold, wet, tired, frustrated and hungry. You will fall on the easiest bunny hill, and then after you've mastered techniques on the easy runs, you'll go to a more difficult run, and be clumsy all over again. Be patient. It keeps getting more fun the better you get, honest. The more mileage you get, the better your turns become . . . keep riding!

Before you make your big debut on the hill, remember to laugh at yourself. Learning a new sport can be humiliating if you don't let your teeth show once in a while. If you're an expert double black diamond skier, swallow your pride while executing face plants and generally looking klutzy on the bunny hill. Keep your attitude adjusted and those bumpy first days will be a laugh later on.

FIG. 5: USE OF ZEN ON THE SLOPES

IF YOU'RE LIKE MOST FOLKS, YOU WANT TO JUMP ON THE BOARD AND GO! NOT SO FAST! THERE ARE SOME BASICS WE HAVE TO COVER FIRST

SNOWBOARDING LINGO:

As with other sports, snowboarding has its own specialized lingo. With it, snowboarders describe their equipment and maneuvers, the conditions and terrain on which they ride, as well as the degree of snowboarding prowess (or lack thereof) displayed by themselves or other snowboarders. This lingo can often be so specialized as to border on being a foreign language. So, if you overhear someone saying, "Way rad, this totally aggro dudette tweaked catching air during a shred session in the halfpipe," don't worry! You haven't been beamed to another planet! These are humans speaking their own special brand of English. If you ask them something simple like directions to the restrooms, they'll probably give you an answer you can understand. However, if you ask them to explain the workings of their equipment, you'll probably get totally lost.

Hence, the importance of learning snowboard-speak! To learn from other riders and snowboard instructors, you'll have to know the lingo. In the next few pages I'll go over the most important snowboard terms. Learn them and you'll be able to communicate with and learn from other snowboarders, as well as understand the rest of this book.

LINGO TO MAKE YOU SOUND COOL:

Snowboarders love to describe each other in ways that mere mortals can't understand. The terms they devise to do this aren't always necessary since there are often perfectly suitable descriptive terms already in general usage. But using words everyone already knows doesn't do anything to make the speaker sound cool or add an air of mystery to the sport. New words are required!

Some of these new terms actually have their roots in the English language. For instance, to be "aggro" with the snowboard means to perform aggressively. To be "rad" is to be radical. To "tweak" is to twist or bend. To "shred" means to ride down the hill in an aggro fashion.

Then there are terms which are totally fabricated, seemingly in an effort to break every spelling rule your poor old English teacher managed to teach you.

"Gnarly," which means good, bad (but only in the sense that bad and good are interchangeable these days), rad, aggro or tough, is such a term.

Then, to really snub your nose at your old English teacher, you can say stuff like, "Way rad, like, totally gnarly, man, totally!" which means good or bad, as the case may be. Just make sure he or she is not behind you in the lift line when you say it!

LINGO TO LEARN BY:

Far more important than learning the lingo to make you sound hip is learning the lingo that will enable you to learn the sport of snowboarding. One of the first things to learn is what to call the different parts of a snowboard, as well as what they're supposed to do, and not supposed to do.

TIP: The turned-up end of the board which generally goes down the hill first, especially given intermediate or advanced riders. For beginners, as we'll learn, it's sometimes pot luck.

TAIL: The end of the board which generally travels down the hill following the tip. The tail is also turned up, which keeps it from digging in the snow when the rider is riding backward, or doing

tricks. But gee, that sounds a lot like the description of the tip! Kind of confusing for beginners! Just remember, the tip is usually more pointed than the tail. Resist the temptation to stencil "tip" and "tail" at appropriate locations on your board since it's a dead giveaway when you're trying to look like an expert in the lodge.

SIDECUT: Refers to the longitudinal change in the width of the board. If you look at a board from above, you'll notice that the center of the board is narrower than the tip and tail. That's sidecut. Sidecut helps in turning. The deeper the sidecut, the tighter the turn radius can be.

CAMBER: The tip-to-tail arc built into the board. Camber, along with sidecut, aids in turning. When the center of your board (where the camber is) is pressured with your weight, the arc is reversed to carve turns.

EDGE: The edges run from tip to tail on the bottom of the board, one on each side, and are generally made of steel. Your edges enable the board to carve turns in packed snow without losing traction.

FIG. 7: SNOWBOARDING LINGO

Zen and the Art of Snowboarding

BASE: This is the flat bottom surface of the snowboard. A good base will glide smoothly over the snow.

BINDINGS: These are the devices that secure your feet to the board. There are two basic types, highback and plate bindings. The highback binding is primarily plastic, with straps across your feet and ankles and a rigid padded support that fits against your calf. This type of binding offers support to ankles and calves when turning. The plate binding is usually a metal plate, as the name implies, shaped like the bottom of your boot, with attachments at the toe and heel. These are made for specialized snowboard boots.

LEASH: A nylon strap about an inch wide, one end of which is attached to the front binding or the board and the other end of which is always secured to you—on your forward leg when riding or your wrist if you are carrying the board on a slope. ALWAYS USE YOUR LEASH! If your board gets away from you on a slope, it could hurt somebody, who may in turn want to hurt you! Be cool, use your leash!

NONSKID PAD: These are textured areas on the top of the board. They are positioned in front of the back binding

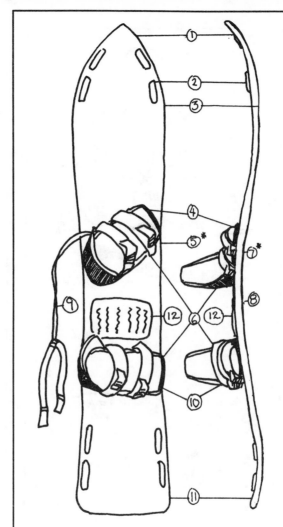

SNOWBOARD ANATOMY

1. TIP (NOSE, BOW)
2. TRACTION PADS
3. EDGE (RAIL)
4. FORWARD FOOT POSITION
5. SIDE CUT
6. HIGHBACK BINDING
7. CAMBER
8. BASE
9. LEASH
10. BACK FOOT POSITION
11. TAIL (END, BACK)
12. NON-SKID PAD

* SIDECUT AND CAMBER EXAGGERATED

FIG. 8: PARTS OF THE SNOWBOARD

and keep your back foot from slipping off the board when you're performing simple maneuvers without having your foot fastened into the binding.

TRACTION PADS: These are textured bits of self-adhesive neoprene which give you added grip when you grab the board while doing tricks.

SNOWBOARD ACCESSORIES AND WHAT THEY DO:

Okay, so much for the board itself. But it turns out there's more to learn. How do you attach yourself to the board? Stay warm and dry? Look cool? Well read on!

BOOTS: The snowboard boots you select are vital pieces of equipment. They, along with your bindings, will connect you to your board and greatly influence your control over it. They will also keep your feet warm and dry. There are two basic types of boots to choose from, soft- and hard-shelled boots.

The hard-shelled boot (fig. 9) consists of a rigid plastic outer shell, a deep-treaded sole and an insulated firm inner liner, similar to a ski boot liner. These boots are hinged at the ankle to give forward flexion and are secured to the board with the use of a binding. They close with buckles or ratchet bales

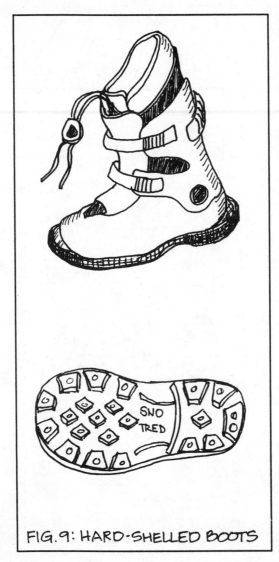

FIG. 9: HARD-SHELLED BOOTS

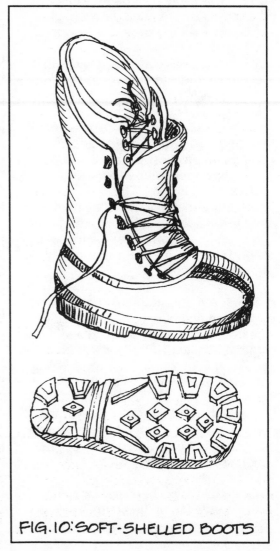

FIG. 10: SOFT-SHELLED BOOTS

like a ski boot. These boots offer the firmest support to your foot and ankle, yet allow some lateral movement. The hard-shelled boot is great for carving turns. Many of the top racers use this type.

The soft-shelled boot (fig. 10) has a soft upper instead of rigid plastic. It also has deeply treaded rubber soles and liners similar to those found in ski boots. Soft-shelled boots provide more flexibility and comfort than their hard-shelled counterparts, but at the expense of some high-speed control. "Freestyle" competitors, who perform acrobatic arrays of twists, turns and jumps, use a soft boot for freedom of movement in any direction.

WESTERN RIDING gives you the advantage of both types of boots. The hard-shelled boot is worn on the front foot for added support, and the soft-shelled boot is worn on the back foot for maximum flex.

PARKA: Your parka is important because it will keep you warm and dry, and it has lots of pockets to carry all the stuff you'll be shlepping around the mountain. The jacket should be insulated, and the outside shell should be made from sturdy wind- and water-resistant fabric. Make sure to get a loose-fitting parka to accommodate layers of warm

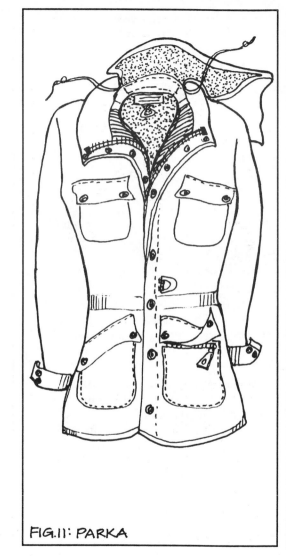

FIG.11: PARKA

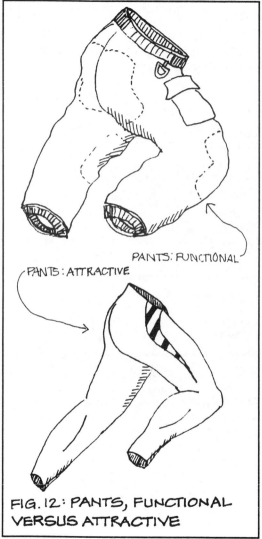

PANTS: FUNCTIONAL

PANTS: ATTRACTIVE

FIG. 12: PANTS, FUNCTIONAL VERSUS ATTRACTIVE

clothing underneath for those extra cold days.

PANTS: The type of pants you wear snowboarding should be able to keep you (hopefully) warm and dry. They should allow for total freedom of movement, so don't buy them too tight no matter how much you think it'll enhance your chances with the opposite sex. There are three types of pants used for snowboarding:

Stretch Pants: These are the ski-type pants which are very good-looking on the right bodies, but offer little insulation and dryness. Remember, you'll be sitting and kneeling in the snow often during the learning process, so go for comfort first and style second.

Snowboard Pants (also called "powder pants" or "warmups"): These are baggy, insulated pants with an outside shell that is water- and wind-resistant with extra padding on the knees and rear end. They are the most comfortable, the most commonly seen on the hill, and by far the least attractive, but, hey, this isn't a fashion show!

Neoprene Pants: These are tight-fitting pants made out of wetsuitlike material. They offer maximum warmth, as well as a bit of "cushion" all over.

These are excellent for learning, providing you're not learning in extremely warm spring weather, since they tend to be too warm when it's not very cool out.

HAT: Keeps your brains warm, so wear one on cold days, or you'll get stupid.

HEADBAND: Keeps your ears warm and generally add to a "cool" appearance.

GLOVES: Keeps your hands and fingers warm and dry. Invest in a good pair that will keep your hands toasty. Cold, wet fingers can ruin your day. If you are prone to cold fingers, try mittens. They're even warmer than gloves. Either gloves or mittens should be insulated and water-repellant. Leather gloves stay wet for days, so avoid them.

SHADES AND GOGGLES: Good sunglasses protect your eyes from the intense and damaging ultraviolet rays present at high altitudes. Quality goggles do the same thing as well as help keep your face warm and protect your eyes from the wind.

SUNSCREEN: Protect your face and lips with sunscreen and moisturizer.

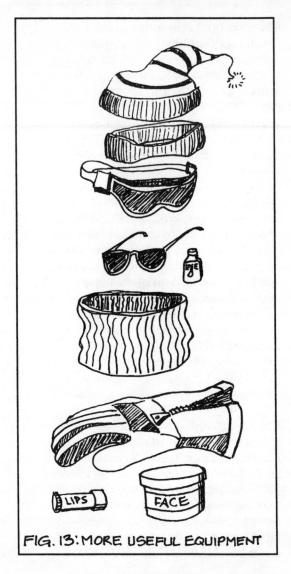

FIG. 13: MORE USEFUL EQUIPMENT

PARTS OF THE SNOWBOARDER

(YOU): Okay, now you know how to sound cool, what to call the thing you ride on and how to refer to the stuff you wear. But in order for you to understand the descriptions of the maneuvers in the chapters that follow, you also need to know how I describe you, the rider, in relation to the board and slope you'll be riding on.

One of the first things you'll have to determine is whether you are a "regular" or a "goofy-foot" rider. To do this, you have to know which is your "front foot" and which is your "back foot." That's easy! Your front foot is the foot you place nearest the front or tip of the board. But you have two feet and only one of them can be at the front of the board. Which one should it be?

In picking which foot to put forward, you will be trying to determine directional stance, or which way you want to stand when you're sideways on a board. If you have experience with other board sports, you already know that one foot will feel more natural forward. Once you decide which way to ride, stick with it. There's nothing more confusing to a beginner than switching foot position halfway through learning the basic maneuvers.

If you've never had to determine which of your feet goes best forward, try these methods:

1. If you skateboard, surf or slalom water ski, use that stance.

2. Stand sideways on a skateboard and roll a few feet. Try not to kill yourself. One foot will feel more natural forward than the other one. Use that as your front foot.

3. Stand in front of someone and get a gentle shove from behind. One foot will move forward to break your fall. Try that as your forward foot on the snowboard. (If you don't manage to break your fall, perhaps you should take up another sport).

4. Play baseball. Your stance at bat is probably the same as would be good for snowboarding.

5. Imagine yourself sliding on ice or a slippery floor in your socks. Try your sliding stance on your snowboard.

Methods to determine your stance have varying degrees of reliability, so if you try them all and still don't know your stance, try a stance out on the snow. If when you ride in this stance, you only feel in control with your board going backward, then you probably have the wrong stance. If your board wants to travel forward (tip first) and you have some control, then you have found your correct stance.

FIG. 14: BEST FOOT FORWARD (IMAGINED)

If you ride with your left foot forward, you're riding in "regular" stance (fig. 15). If you ride with your right foot forward, then you're riding in a "goofy-foot" stance (fig. 16). Remember that for future instructions.

Another thing you'll have to know is which edge of the snowboard you'll want to be riding on. To describe the different edges of the snowboard, I simply refer to them as "toe edge" or "heel edge," depending on whether that particular edge is closest to your toes or your heels when you are buckled into your board. If you ride regular stance, your right edge will be your toe edge and your left edge will be your heel edge. The opposite will be true if you're a "goofy footer."

FIG. 15: RIDING REGULAR FOOT (LEFT FOOT FORWARD)

FIG. 16: RIDING GOOFY FOOT (RIGHT FOOT FORWARD)

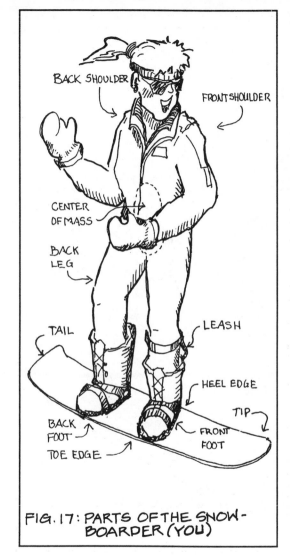

**FIG. 17: PARTS OF THE SNOW-
BOARDER (YOU)**

Labels on figure: BACK SHOULDER, FRONT SHOULDER, CENTER OF MASS, BACK LEG, TAIL, LEASH, HEEL EDGE, TIP, BACK FOOT, FRONT FOOT, TOE EDGE

WHAT TO EXPECT AT THE RESORT

Your first snowboarding experience will probably be at the nearest ski resort, so we should discuss what you'll be encountering at a typical resort. If you have a skiing background, you are already familiar with the customs, etiquette, rules and survival techniques of resort life. If you have never experienced a winter resort, please pay attention.

Now, just exactly what is a ski resort anyway? Well, it will have a mountain or mountains, hopefully with plenty of snow on them, with some sort of mechanical apparatus to get you up the hill. At the bottom of the hill (and sometimes up the hill as well) will be a day lodge. This can vary from a simple shack with benches and picnic tables to palatial multilevel accommodations with fireplaces, decks, breathtaking vistas, with all sorts of shops, restaurants and services. The resort will have a ski patrol for your safety and most likely a ski school (many now have snowboard instructors available).

In the day-lodge area you will almost always find the lift ticket windows, food and drink services, restrooms and rental and repair shops. Accessory, equipment and clothing shops are usually nearby. They are convenient but expensive, so try to remember all your gear.

When you're planning your trip to a ski resort, keep in mind that snowboarding is a relatively new sport to the ski industry. Some resorts don't permit snowboarding at all while others are permitting it on a trial basis, often in restricted areas of the mountain. Some ski areas may require that you take a lesson or demonstrate competence on your board before issuing you a lift ticket. Call ahead to find out, so you won't be disappointed when you get there.

When you arrive at the resort, drive or walk around the area and get a "lay of the land." Find out where the day lodge, shops and restaurants are located. Newsstands at resort areas often have a directory with information (and sometimes discounts) to local attractions, goods and services.

Get a handle on the parking situation if you are traveling by car. Carrying a pile of heavy equipment to the day lodge from a distant parking lot is not the way to start your first snowboarding day. Some resorts offer shuttle service to and from outer parking lots. Another alternative is to drop your gear off at the day lodge the night before. Most areas have coin-operated lockers or overnight storage available to reduce the gear-shlepping problem faced by resort visitors.

The next day, arrive at the day lodge at least an hour earlier than you think you should. It's amazing how long it can take to futz around at the rental shop, ticket windows and day-lodge cafeteria. If you have equipment, it has resale value. Keep it in your view or locked up until you go out on the hill. If you're on a budget or in a hurry, pack a lunch. Food lines can be long, meals usually expensive and their quality inconsistent.

FIG. 18: EXPECT THE UNEXPECTED

Ask the folks at the ticket window about the availability of package deals and discounts. Most resorts offer a good beginner's package that includes both the lesson and lift ticket for one price. If this is not available, ask if they have a lower-mountain lift pass. This pass gives you access to all the slopes you'll need for your first few learning sessions and is often cheaper than a general lift pass. After you get your lift ticket, ask how and where it is to be attached to your clothing. Some resorts get downright picky about how you should wear your pass.

FIG. 19 : EATING AT THE RESORT

MOUNTAIN ETIQUETTE AND RULES OF THE ROAD:

Before you actually get out on the mountain, be sure to familiarize yourself with the rules of the resort. Most ski areas have a set of rules that all guests are expected to obey. Learn and follow the rules at all times, and you can have a great time up on the hill without being a bother or danger to anyone, including yourself.

These rules are encapsulated in the standardized Skier's and Snowboarder's Responsibility Code (fig. 20). You will note that the code just states that you should ski or ride in control and avoid collisions. Pretty good advice, huh? Again, know the rules before you go out on the hill! Follow them and your own common sense and you'll have a great time without becoming a threat.

In addition to resort rules, there are a few general customs that everyone is expected to practice. Some are safety oriented and some are common courtesies. You can make the day pleasant for yourself and everyone around you by practicing the local customs.

FIG. 20: BE SAFETY CONSCIOUS

Zen and the Art of Snowboarding

MOUNTAIN CUSTOMS

1. Make way for vehicles on the slopes. They will usually travel along the edges of the trails. Vehicles you are most likely to see are snowcats (groomers) and snowmobiles.

2. Call out, "On your left!" or "On your right!" when overtaking someone on the slopes. If you hear this warning from behind as you are riding, hold your course and speed, and let him pass on your right or left as he has warned you.

3. When you see someone crash, offer assistance and call the ski patrol if necessary.

4. When you see small children, give them plenty of room, and give them a hand if they are fumbling with gloves or equipment.

5. Reduce your speed and use extra caution in crowded areas.

6. When entering trail intersections, stop and look uphill before proceeding, particularly if you cannot be seen by approaching skiers.

7. Safe mountain driving is a team effort. Assist your driver with clearing icy windshields and lights, digging out the car and installing snowchains, etc. And share the driving.

FIG. 21: YIELD TO VEHICLES ON THE SLOPES

FIG. 22: PLACE MARKERS ABOVE AN ACCIDENT & CALL SKI PATROL

FIG. 23: WINTER DRIVING IS A TEAM EFFORT

TERRAIN AND SNOW CONDITIONS:

The conditions you will be snowboarding in will vary greatly, depending on two main factors: the steepness of the terrain and the actual condition of the snow. The condition of the snow is a result of many variables, including weather, grooming and traffic (skiers and snowboarders).

There are six basic types of snow you will encounter. They are powder, fresh-packed powder, hard pack, moguls, ice and spring conditions. All these conditions can be ridden, but some are more desirable than others, and some you'll want to avoid while you are learning to snowboard. Read on and you'll see what I mean.

TYPES OF SNOW:

POWDER: The stuff dreams are made of—cold, dry, fluffy, chest-high clouds of snow. Riding in powder is the ultimate choice for snowboarding, but use caution in the beginning. Powder causes more drag on your board than when you're riding in other conditions. It can bog you down if it's too deep or you're not on steep enough terrain. Start out in a few inches, then a few more, then start riding in a foot or two.

FRESH-PACKED POWDER: This is ideal for learning. The snow is freshly fallen and packed by snowcats towing rollers behind them. It is soft enough that your falls are relatively painless and firm enough to keep you moving down the hill without bogging down.

HARD PACK: Hard pack is perhaps the most common condition. This is where the snow is several days old and packed down by people skiing over it. In this condition, it's pretty hard and not real nice to fall on. (This is where neoprene or padded snowboard pants come in handy.) You will gain speed much more quickly on hard pack than on powder or fresh-packed powder, given the same slope steepness.

MOGULS (bumps): These are mounds of snow found on ungroomed intermediate and advanced runs. They are carved into the snowpack by the skiers and riders as they repeat regular rounded turns down the trail. Gracefully maneuvering through a steep mogul field is a real challenge for expert riders. Stay out of the bumps until you have mastered all the basic techniques and can perform them on fairly steep terrain. If you make a wrong turn and find yourself stranded in a mogul field, take your board off, attach your leash to your wrist, and walk (or crawl) out of it. Walk along the edge of the run to avoid collisions with skiers or other snowboarders.

ICE: Ice occurs when hard pack continues to be skied over with no new snowfall or if water gets on the snow, either by surface melting, rain or other causes (springs, creeks, etc.) and it freezes. Ice is really fast to ride on, it's difficult to turn on and it's terrible to fall on. As a beginning to intermediate snowboarder, you'll want to avoid ice.

SPRING CONDITIONS (also known as crud, corn, mud or slush): This is a widely varying condition caused by daily thawing and nightly freezing of the snowpack. The snow ranges anywhere from ice in the morning to mud puddles and streams in the afternoon. Spring conditions change many times during the day and from run to run. For instance, you may take a fast run down an icy trail, then suddenly find yourself bogged down in slow slushy snow as you move down in elevation on the slope. This slush may suddenly turn to mud, dirt, rocks, tree stumps, running streams or ponds, all referred to as "obstacles" in the morning snow-condition reports. Use extra caution when riding in spring conditions.

FIG. 24: POWDER!

FIG. 25: SPRING CONDITIONS

DESCRIBING THE TERRAIN:

Ski runs—the terrain you will be learning to snowboard on—are classified into four basic categories according to the slope angle and degree of difficulty relative to the mountain. The four categories are: EASIEST, MORE DIFFICULT, MOST DIFFICULT, and EXPERT ONLY. Remember, these four categories are relative to the particular mountain. An intermediate run on "ANY SMALL MOUNTAIN USA" may be cake for you, while the intermediate run on "ALPEN MOUNTAIN BIG SWISS" may be a death ride to hell. Warm up on easier terrain if you're not familiar with the mountain. Get an idea of what they really mean by "EASY WAY DOWN" before you point your board down there.

EASIEST WAY DOWN: These trails are marked by signs with a large green circle on them (fig. 26). Most of these runs will be located on the lower part of the mountain. They are maintained for you, the beginner and intermediate riders. The slope angle is the smallest on the mountain. This easy terrain keeps you from picking up too much speed while you're learning. The trails are usually wide, so that you have plenty of room to maneuver, and machine-groomed so that the snow surface is relatively smooth.

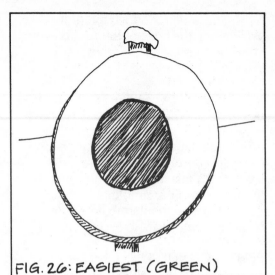

FIG. 26: EASIEST (GREEN)

FIG. 27: MORE DIFFICULT (BLUE)

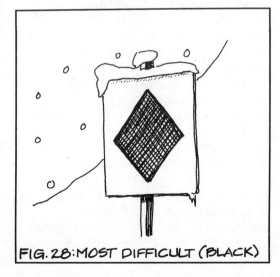

FIG. 28: MOST DIFFICULT (BLACK)

FIG. 29: EXPERT ONLY (BLACK)

Zen and the Art of Snowboarding

MORE DIFFICULT: Signs with a large blue square signify the intermediate runs. Most of them will be located mid-mountain and will be anywhere from pretty easy to pretty scary. Again, familiarize yourself with the mountain. Ask which is the easiest or hardest "more difficult way down." Blue trails will often be narrower and always be steeper than the green trails. Some are groomed, some "bumped out" with moguls.

MOST DIFFICULT: These are the runs marked by a black diamond on the trail marking sign; they are found at or near the top of the mountain. Get comfortable on the blues before you consider hitting the blacks or you're in for one wild ride. It's up here that you'll find the big mogul fields with names like "Devil's Alley," "Maniac" and "Psycho." The names give fair warning to what lies ahead. They can be very steep, narrow and have huge moguls. To enjoy this stuff, you have to be a good, strong rider.

EXPERT ONLY: These runs are also found at or near the top of the mountain, with two black diamonds on the sign. Forget them for now if you're at the beginning or intermediate level. They are the steepest of the steeps. Snow defies gravity by sticking to these suckers. You will not only have a lousy time trying to flounder down them as a beginner, but you will most likely become a dangerous projectile flying down the hill. Boarding down an "Expert Only" run should be a goal for a very advanced rider.

CHAPTER THREE: GETTING STARTED

NOW THAT YOU KNOW YOUR BASIC LINGO & THEORY, IT'S TIME TO PUT THAT KNOWLEDGE TO WORK ON THE SLOPES!

PICKING A PLACE TO START:
Your first attempt at snowboarding can range anywhere from a merry frolic in the snow to the worst day of your life. To improve your chances of experiencing the former of these two scenarios, be particular about the place you choose to start. Try to get one that has the following features (fig. 30):

PROPER TERRAIN: Within easy walking distance of the day lodge and the bar, look for a gentle slope with approximately a 15 degree pitch and a large runnout or flat area below. The hill should have a constant single fall line, which means the hill slopes in only one constant direction.

SNOW: An absolute necessity. As we discussed, the best snow is freshly packed powder, that is, a foot of new snow, smashed, rolled and smoothed out by the snowcats during the night while you were dreaming of shredding the slopes. Fresh cat-rolled tracks will leave the surface of the slope looking like corduroy. Packed powder makes an ideal "crash-landing" pad. Old snow can get pretty hard, even icy, so if you can pick your day, try for one just after a good dump of snow (at least 6 to 12 inches, a foot is ideal) after the groomers have done their thing.

CLEAR RUNOUT: A runout is the flat area below the slope. Make sure it is long enough to stop easily, and is completely free of obstacles. A tree or lost doggie at the bottom seems to act as a magnet for beginners, and you will be inextricably drawn to it. Trees hurt, doggies bite. Go for no obstacles!

LITTLE OR NO TRAFFIC: The most inviting slope will probably be a busy ski run. Resist the urge. You have enough to concentrate on without the distraction of dodging passing skiers. You, as a beginner on a busy ski run, are an irritating obstacle for the more experienced skiers and snowboarders. Be nice and try to find another area. You will understand this when you have become experienced and have to duck and dodge some beginner making erratic turns, stops and falls in front of you.

GOOD WEATHER: Try for a clear, calm day with temperatures in the 30's and 40's. It will be much simpler to learn maneuvers if you don't have to concern yourself with the worsening blizzard, foggy goggles, losing your hat, and sub-Arctic windchill factors.

Your chances of getting the ideal learning location will be greater if you take a lesson. The instructors usually have a place staked out with ideal terrain for beginners.

PRECAUTIONS:

There are a few things you should consider before you go out on the mountain. You don't want to be a conspicuous flatlander, nor do you want to hurt yourself or another fun-seeker up there. Here are some simple precautions to make sure you accomplish those goals.

First, as we've said before, pick the proper terrain. Start in the flats, then gradually work your way up to steeper slopes. The higher you go and the steeper the hill, the faster you'll slide down. Only after you've mastered the skills of turning and stopping on easy runs should you move up to steeper stuff. Your maneuvers will be more difficult or even impossible to perform if you have advanced to a run that is too

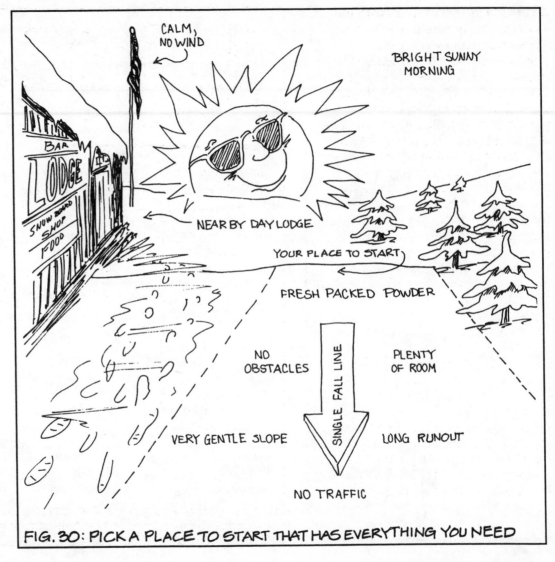

FIG. 30: PICK A PLACE TO START THAT HAS EVERYTHING YOU NEED

steep. Don't try to keep up with the way-rad shredders until you're ready. Advance at your own speed.

Before you actually go out on the mountain, always check your equipment. Look for any obviously broken, cracked or wiggly parts. It's a looooong hike down to the shop if your binding unmounts itself at the top of the chairlift. If anything looks suspicious, have an expert check your equipment.

Board with a buddy, particularly if you are boarding in the back country, deep powder or the trees. If you do get yourself into trouble, your friend can go for help. Buddies are also useful for borrowing lunch money, letting you know when your face is getting frostbitten and providing company on the lift rides.

One last precaution: Avoid collisions at all costs! They often cause injuries. Avoiding collisions requires riding in control at all times and awareness. Don't stare down at your board. Look up at the traffic and merge onto a slope just as you would a busy freeway. Watch where you are going. If you can't turn or stop in time to avoid a tree, skier or other obstacle, SIT DOWN! The butt drop works as an emergency brake.

FIG. 31: SNOWBOARD INSTRUCTORS WILL HAVE THE BEST NOVICE TERRAIN STAKED OUT

THE THEORY OF SNOWBOARDING:

Okay, now that you know the lingo and you've picked a place to start, we can start snowboarding, right? Well, before you actually get out on the slopes, you need to go over a little theory. Now don't skip this section! Learning the theory behind snowboarding, as dull as it might sound, will reap you endless benefits out on the hill. It will save you from repeated mistakes and much frustration. You'll be able to think through the maneuvers you attempt and analyze what you're doing, be it right or wrong. If you take the time to learn about "weight distribution" and "edge pressure," chances are much better you'll be able to successfully ride down the hill instead of performing an endless string of "face plants" to get to the bottom.

THE FALL LINE (NO PUN INTENDED):

This is perhaps one of the most important concepts in all of beginning snowboarding. Make sure you understand it fully! The fall line is the greatest angle of slope from any point on a hill. To determine exactly where it is, imagine yourself at the top of a hill with a ball. Let the ball roll down. Gravity will take it down the greatest angle of the slope. (the steepest and most direct way down). This path is the fall line (fig. 32). There is at least one fall line from any

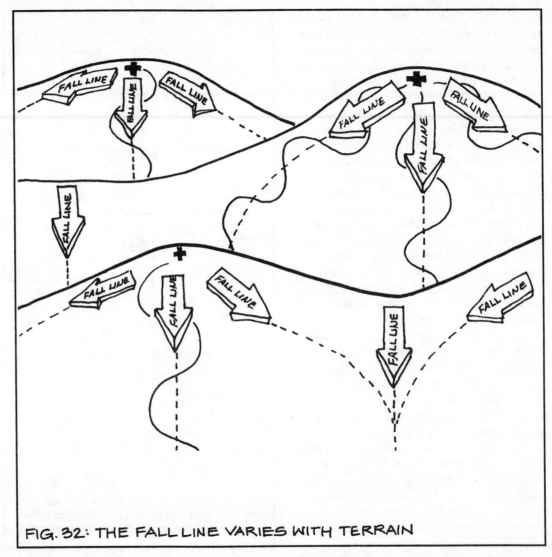

FIG. 32: THE FALL LINE VARIES WITH TERRAIN

point on a hill, and the line is not always straight. All snowboarding is done on slopes of varying degrees. The direction of travel is down the slope, and to get there you'll be turning back and forth across the fall line. The reason it's so important to know where the fall line is on a hill is that by maneuvering the board in relation to the fall line, you make the board go, turn and stop—three things you'll want to know how to do (especially stop!). Not knowing where the fall line is will cause you to do things like riding down the hill out of control (not cool), riding down the hill backward out of control (less cool) or performing maneuvers like the "face christie" (way uncool). Always know where the fall line is!

CENTER OF MASS (CM):

When riding a snowboard, you maintain control by manipulating your body weight in relation to it. As we all learned in junior high school, weight is the result of mass being acted upon by a gravitational force. Hence, by locating your body's mass properly in relation to the snowboard, you maintain control. (Assuming, of course, that you'll be snowboarding under the influence of gravity. If you plan to snowboard in outer space, you'll need another book.)

For these reasons you're going to be

FIG. 33: WHEN YOUR WEIGHT IS OVER YOUR FRONT FOOT, YOUR BOARD WILL GO DOWNHILL FORWARD

FIG. 34: WHEN YOUR WEIGHT IS TOO FAR BACK (OVER YOUR BACK FOOT) YOUR BOARD WILL GO DOWNHILL BACKWARD

concerned with the location of your body weight, or mass, when you're snowboarding. In snowboarding lingo, you'll be concerned with your body's Center of Mass (CM) in relation to the board. CM is different from just plain mass in that it is the imaginary focal point of all the gravitational forces acting upon a body, in this case, yours. For the purposes of learning to snowboard, you can consider your CM to reside in the lower region of your torso, near the stomach. So, when I ask you to move your CM to a certain position, you'll want to slide your torso to that position. Note that moving your CM around is not very efficiently accomplished by bending at the waist and leaning. Instead, imagine sliding your hips around— forward, back and side to side. Your torso follows much more efficiently, no?

Always be aware of your CM in relation to the board!! Why is this important? Well, the portion of the board over which your CM resides will be the portion of the board which travels down the hill first. When your CM is forward, you are weighting or applying pressure to your front foot. When you do this, your board will pivot until this weighted end (the front or tip) is pointing directly down the fall line. The board will travel forward, tip first, as long as your CM

remains over your front foot (fig. 33).

The opposite is also true. If you weight the tail of your board, it will pivot until you're traveling straight down the fall line tail first (fig. 34). Not good! But even worse, consider what happens if you can't resist the natural beginner's urge to lean back when riding to stop or control the board. You don't stop! You simply turn around and start sailing down the hill backward! Not properly controlling your CM in relation to the board IS THE MOST COMMON BEGINNER'S ERROR and can be very frustrating. Always be aware of your CM in relation to the board! If your board doesn't want to cooperate by traveling down the hill forward (tip first), consider your CM. Is it over your front foot? Most likely it is not. If you are having trouble controlling your CM, remember to check the placement of your hips. By moving your hips over the front foot, your weight will shift forward with them and your board should go forward.

THEORY OF TURNING:

Turning is what learning to snowboard is all about. Turns allow you to steer the board where you want it to go and at the speed you want to travel. Every time you turn, your board slows down. After you finish the turn you steer downhill again and pick up momentum. The object is to execute a precise, elegant movement through the turn with an economy of motion.

Okay, but exactly how do you turn? Imagine yourself traveling directly down the fall line with your CM centered over your front foot. You're picking up speed and want to turn to slow yourself down. To turn, you must accomplish three motions simultaneously: you must pivot the board, shift your weight and pressure the edge of your board (either toe edge or heel edge, depending on how you are turning).

To pivot the board, you kick your back foot either backward or forward, depending on which way you want to turn. As you pivot, you have to gradually begin to shift some additional weight to your back foot. At the same time, you should begin to pressure the uphill edge of your board (either toe edge or heel edge) to begin riding that edge.

Doing all this will cause you to begin to turn from riding directly down the fall line toward riding perpendicular to the fall line. As you approach riding perpendicular to the fall line, you should continue to shift weight to your back foot so that as you begin to ride perpendicular to the fall line, your weight is equally distributed over both feet. At the same time, apply more pressure to the uphill edge of the board so that you ride that edge more.

To turn so that you are again traveling down the fall line, you simply reverse the procedure: shift your weight forward and release edge pressure. Presto! It's back down the fall line to set up for another turn.

It's very important that you concentrate on your weight shifts during turning. For the most part, you need most of your weight over your front foot. You only have your weight equally distributed over both feet while you are actually perpendicular to the fall line. Otherwise, KEEP YOUR WEIGHT FORWARD. Otherwise learning to turn will be an impossible nightmare.

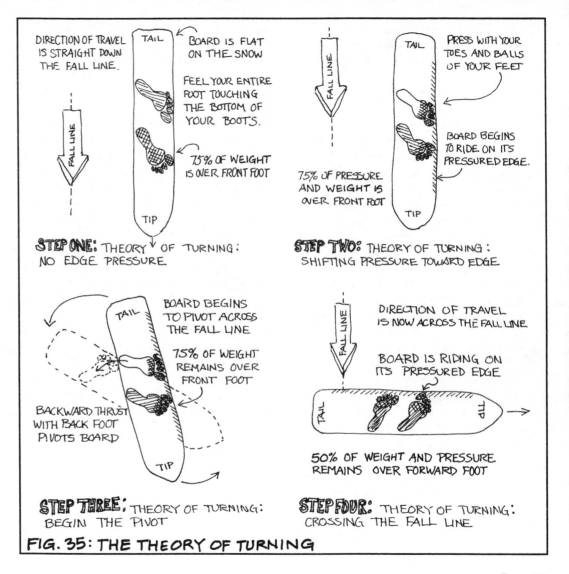

DIRECTION OF TRAVEL IS STRAIGHT DOWN THE FALL LINE.
TAIL
BOARD IS FLAT ON THE SNOW
FEEL YOUR ENTIRE FOOT TOUCHING THE BOTTOM OF YOUR BOOTS.
FALL LINE
75% OF WEIGHT IS OVER FRONT FOOT
TIP

STEP ONE: THEORY OF TURNING: NO EDGE PRESSURE.

FALL LINE
TAIL
PRESS WITH YOUR TOES AND BALLS OF YOUR FEET
BOARD BEGINS TO RIDE ON ITS PRESSURED EDGE.
75% OF PRESSURE AND WEIGHT IS OVER FRONT FOOT
TIP

STEP TWO: THEORY OF TURNING: SHIFTING PRESSURE TOWARD EDGE

TAIL
BOARD BEGINS TO PIVOT ACROSS THE FALL LINE
75% OF WEIGHT REMAINS OVER FRONT FOOT
BACKWARD THRUST WITH BACK FOOT PIVOTS BOARD
TIP

STEP THREE: THEORY OF TURNING: BEGIN THE PIVOT

DIRECTION OF TRAVEL IS NOW ACROSS THE FALL LINE
FALL LINE
BOARD IS RIDING ON ITS PRESSURED EDGE
TAIL
TIP
50% OF WEIGHT AND PRESSURE REMAINS OVER FORWARD FOOT

STEP FOUR: THEORY OF TURNING: CROSSING THE FALL LINE

FIG. 35: THE THEORY OF TURNING

FIG. 36: EXECUTING PROPER TURNS

FIG. 37: EXECUTING IMPROPER TURNS

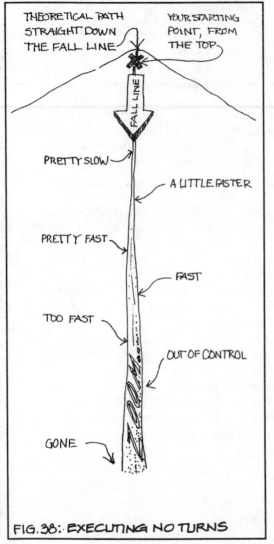

FIG. 38: EXECUTING NO TURNS

Zen and the Art of Snowboarding

BASIC MANEUVERS:

ON FLAT TERRAIN: Okay, you've read about theory, and, of course, before you actually get out on the slopes, you will have read this section. It's a beautiful day, and you're well rested and full of anticipation. Let's start snowboarding!

First, you'll have to walk to your carefully chosen starting place. Let me give you a couple of hints. When carrying your board, carry it under your arm, with the base of the board toward your body and bindings facing away and the tip slightly higher than the tail. Be careful carrying your board through crowded areas. Check for pedestrians at close range before you pivot around to see who's calling your name.

All right, now you are standing at the bottom of the starting area ready to hike to the top and shred down. Hold it! Freeze! There are a few things you have to practice down here in the flats before you climb the bunny hill.

BUCKLING IN: The first thing you'll have to do is buckle into the board. First, sit down with your board across the fall line in front of and downhill from you, with the tip toward your front foot and the tail toward your back foot. (Since you're on flat ground, you'll have to imagine there's a slope and a fall line.) Attach the leash to your front leg

FIG. 39: BE CAREFUL WALKING IN CROWDS

FIG. 40: BUCKLE IN FRONT FOOT

below the knee, near the top of your boot. Clear the snow from the bottom of your front boot and from the inside of your front binding. Buckle in your front foot only (fig. 40). If you have plate bindings, put your toe in the bale first, then attach the heel. If you have high back bindings, buckle the ankle strap first, then the toe strap.

Here's how to tell if you've got it right. Toe and ankle straps should be snug. How snug? Stand up and flex your knee and ankle, then extend them. If your boots are properly laced or buckled, you should have little (less than 1/4 inch) or no lifting of your heel from the bottom of your boot. If your bindings are secured correctly, the bottom of the boot should not lift at all from the binding.

Don't buckle in so tight that you cut off the circulation to your foot. You should be able to wiggle your toes. You'll know if you are buckled or laced in too tight within a few minutes. Your foot will go numb or start screaming OOOOWWW! Try the buckle a notch or two looser.

FALLING AND GETTING UP: As I've said, you'll spend a lot of time falling and getting up while you're learning to snowboard, so falling and getting up is one of the first things to learn. I'll explain how to do this on a hill, but since you're on flat ground right now, you'll just have to imagine a slope and a fall line.

Falling will come naturally. You just have to learn to fall without hurting yourself. This is generally accomplished by breaking your fall with your knees or butt before you try to break your fall with your hands. If you must use your hands, don't lock your arms. Keep them flexed and try to keep your hands in a fist. Don't worry about setting aside time to practice falling. You'll get plenty of practice.

Getting up can be difficult and exhausting. You want to save your energy for snowboarding, not waste it all struggling and floundering trying to stand up. Economy and efficiency of motion are important when you have to pick yourself up twenty or thirty times in one day.

Here's how to stand up like the big dogs (figs. 41-43): It's a piece of cake if you know what to do. Ootch around until you are sitting up, with the board below you (downhill). Keep the board perpendicular to the fall line and ootch yourself down so that your legs are bent and your butt is almost on the board. With your front hand grasp your front leg behind the knee. Then use your arm and leg strength to lift the tip of the board. Keep the tail down and dig into the snow. Cartwheel the tip of the board over the tail as you roll your whole body over until you end up on your hands and knees. (If you originally landed in this position, you can skip the rolling over part.) You should now be kneeling facing up hill, with the board perpendicular to the fall line below you and with the toe edge on the snow. Dig in your toe edge and walk your hands toward your board. Steady yourself with your hands, shift your weight forward over your front foot, then push yourself to a standing position with your lead hand.

STEP ONE

LIFT TIP UP AND PIVOT ON THE TAIL. ROLL YOUR KNEES DOWN TO THE SNOW AS THE TIP COMES UP.

FIG. 41: ASSUME STARTING POSITION

STEP TWO

ROLL THE TIP ALL THE WAY OVER SO THAT IT'S POINTING THE OPPOSITE DIRECTION AS WHEN YOU STARTED

ROLL YOUR BODY OVER WITH THE BOARD. DIG THE EDGE OF YOUR BOARD INTO THE SNOW FOR STABILITY.

FIG. 42: ROLL OVER

STEP THREE

FACING UPHILL FROM A KNEELING POSITION, WALK YOUR HANDS DOWNHILL TOWARD YOUR BOARD AND STAND UP

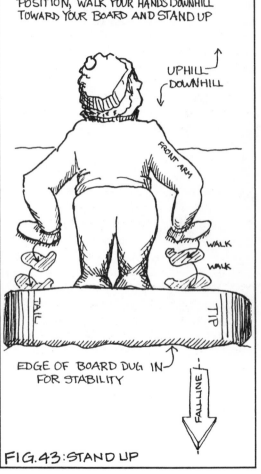

EDGE OF BOARD DUG IN FOR STABILITY

FIG. 43: STAND UP

GET USED TO YOUR BOARD: Now that your front foot is buckled in and you're standing up, try to get used to having that board strapped on your foot. The more time you spend with it this way, the less awkward it will feel. Try lifting one foot, then the other (fig. 44). March in place. Try it with your free foot behind the board and in front.

FIG. 44: KEEP THE BOARD LEVEL & PRACTICE LIFTING IT BOTH IN FRONT AND IN BACK OF YOUR FREE FOOT

WALKING YOUR BOARD (figs. 45-46): Now that you're balanced on the board, let's try moving around on flat terrain. Stand on your free foot and slide your board forward a few inches, then step forward with your free foot. Take small steps at first until you get the hang of it. This is called walking your board and helps to get you where you want to go without the hassle of unbuckling your front foot.

FIG. 45: AT FIRST, TAKE SMALL STEPS & GLIDES ON FLAT TERRAIN

FIG. 46: LEARN TO PUSH YOUR BOARD FROM BEHIND AND IN FRONT

SKATING AND SIDESTEPPING: An alternative to walking the board is skating it. Skating is like walking the board except that you allow the board to glide a little. To skate, you should be standing with your leash on your front leg, front foot buckled in snug, with your back foot standing on the snow. Let's go! Push off with your back foot as you would a skateboard or scooter. Once you've pushed off, step onto the board with your back foot. Keep your weight over your front foot and try to steer the board in a straight line. Take small steps and glides at first. Keep your knees close together and your free back foot on the nonskid pad as you glide. Keep your back straight. Okay, easy so far, huh? Let's go on.

Once you have your balance skating in a straight line, try skating your board around in a big circle. Keep practicing until you can skate the board around in big and small circles in both directions, and with the free foot pushing from the toe and heel side of your board. Are you dizzy yet?

Skating, you will find, will become more and more difficult as the slope of the hill becomes steeper until it finally becomes impossible. When this happens, you'll have to know how to sidestep (fig. 47). First you stand facing

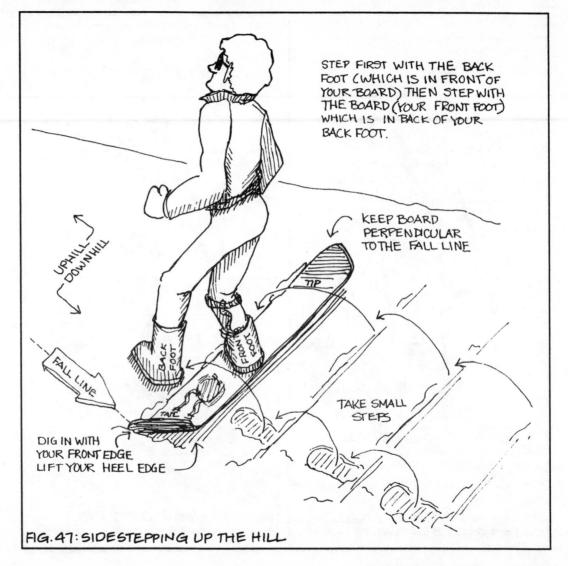

STEP FIRST WITH THE BACK FOOT (WHICH IS IN FRONT OF YOUR BOARD) THEN STEP WITH THE BOARD (YOUR FRONT FOOT) WHICH IS IN BACK OF YOUR BACK FOOT.

KEEP BOARD PERPENDICULAR TO THE FALL LINE

UPHILL DOWNHILL

FALL LINE

TIP

BACK FOOT

FRONT FOOT

TAIL

DIG IN WITH YOUR FRONT EDGE LIFT YOUR HEEL EDGE

TAKE SMALL STEPS

FIG. 47: SIDESTEPPING UP THE HILL

uphill. The board must be exactly perpendicular to the fall line. Keep your free back foot in front of (uphill from) the uphill edge (toe edge) of your board. Dig the toe side edge of your board into the snow by pressuring your front foot toes and lifting your heel edge. Your knees and ankles should be bent. Step up hill with the free back foot (which is actually in front of your front foot now) and pick up the board with your front foot (which is actually behind your back foot), keeping the board perpendicular to the fall line and behind your front foot. Set the board down right behind your free back foot and dig in your toe edge again. Take small steps at first, until you get the hang of it.

Make sure you keep the board perpendicular to the fall line! If you don't, you'll know it right away because your board will take off down the hill (either tip or tail first, depending, which end is lowest on the hill) every time you pick up your back foot.

THE WALKING PIVOT: As fate will have it, when you decide to walk, skate or sidestep your board, you'll be facing in the wrong direction about 50 percent of the time. What to do? The walking pivot! This is done by lifting your board up, turning it and putting it down again (fig. 48). First, pick up your board by

STEP ONE

LIFT BOARD UP KEEPING IT LEVEL

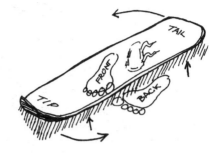

WALKING PIVOT STARTING POSITION

STEP TWO

PIVOT BOARD IN THE AIR AND SET IT DOWN IN FRONT OF YOUR FREE (OR BACK) FOOT.

AT THE SAME TIME, PIVOT ON BACK FOOT

WALKING PIVOT IN PROGRESS

STEP THREE

REPEAT STEPS ONE AND TWO IN THE SAME DIRECTION

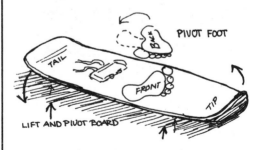

WALKING PIVOT IN PROGRESS

STEP FOUR

THAT'S IT! YOU HAVE NOW TURNED 180 DEGREES. NOW DO IT IN THE OPPOSITE DIRECTION

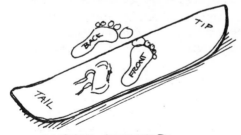

WALKING PIVOT COMPLETED

FIG. 48: THE WALKING PIVOT

bending the knee of your front foot. Keep the bottom of the board parallel to the ground. Put it down and try it again a few times. Once you feel comfortable and balanced picking it up and putting it down in the same place, try this: Lift the board with your front foot and set it back down in front of and perpendicular to your back foot. Pivot on your back foot, then pick the board up again and set it down in front of and perpendicular to your back foot again. You should be 180 degrees from where you started. Practice by making several walking pivots in each direction.

STATIC PIVOTS: These are done with your back foot buckled in, so sit down, buckle in and then get up. Move your hips (your CM, remember) over your front foot, keeping your back straight. Pick out a stationary object directly in front of your board (a tree or a building) and keep your lead shoulder or arm pointed toward it. Hold your arms out away from your body for balance. Bend at your knees, especially your front knee. Do you feel stupid and conspicuous standing there like that? Don't! With the grace of a gazelle, as if you were gently kicking a ball, kick your back foot forward a few inches. This will cause the board to pivot at your front foot and the back of the board to move out in front of you. Now try to pivot the board in the opposite direction so that the tail of the board pivots behind you. Kick your back foot as if you were passing a ball to someone behind you. You should have made tracks in the snow that look like giant "X" marks. Practice the static pivot forward and backward until you have a whole bunch of "X" tracks and can do them without falling over.

Complete control of your board on flat terrain will give you lift line poise and confidence as you go on to more challenging maneuvers on the hill. You'll need to know these drills to learn to turn and to approach and move along lift lines. (A lift line is a maze of poles, ropes, fences and people that you will have to maneuver over, under, around, and through to get a ride up the hill.) Keep practicing these exercises on flat terrain until they're very familiar. Then go on to the bunny hill.

BASIC DOWNHILL MANEUVERS: THE STRAIGHT GLIDE (fig. 49):

Okay, it's time to snowboard! Using the techniques we've discussed (skating and sidestepping), go 30 yards or so up the hill but not to where it gets too steep. Your first straight glide down the hill should be on a gentle slope. Otherwise you might pick up too much speed (we haven't learned to stop yet!), so the hill should be gentle enough that you won't be scared to go straight down and coast to a stop on the runout. If it's too steep, look for an easier one or start from lower on the hill.

The first thing you have to do is get your board pivoted around (right now it's perpendicular to the fall line) so that it's pointed down the fall line. To do this, first point down the fall line with your lead arm. Place your back foot on the nonskid pad. Flex your legs, move your hips forward and keep your weight over your front foot. Your board should pivot into the fall line and start gliding down the hill. Keep your shoulders squared to the board and your head up. Look where you want to go.

When you start gliding downhill, resist the urge to stare down at your board or lean back, two very common beginner boo-boos. GET AGGRO! Stay flexed and stay forward. After you glide straight to the bottom you should coast to a stop on the runout. If you need to stop sooner, you can step off your board with your back foot. In an emergency, you can stop by sitting down and engaging your emergency brake (fig. 50).

Practice the straight glide until you can go down the hill without falling over and with some semblance of balance, then try it with both feet buckled into your bindings. Once you've got it, go all the way to the top of this bunny hill and try some sliding pivots.

SLIDING PIVOTS: These are just like the static pivots you did down on the flats, except now you do them while you're gliding down the fall line. Start down the hill in a straight glide, then pivot your board back and forth across the fall line. You should have completed several sliding pivots by the time you reach the bottom of the bunny hill. Remember to keep your legs flexed, and whatever you do, don't lean back!

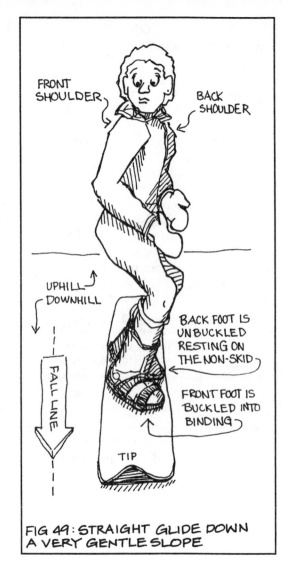

FIG 49: STRAIGHT GLIDE DOWN A VERY GENTLE SLOPE

FIG. 50: AS A LAST RESORT, YOU CAN USE YOUR 'EMERGENCY BRAKE'

SIDESLIPPING (figs. 51-52): This maneuver can be a lifesaver in steeper terrain because with it you can control your speed. Practicing it will also help you "find your edges," that is, the balance point between too much edge pressure and not enough. Sideslipping will also teach you what makes the board stop; it will also help you understand a flat board verses an edged board.

Okay, get to the top of the hill, sit down and buckle both feet in for this one, with the board, as usual, perpendicular to the fall line. Your back foot should be as snug as your front foot in the binding. Stand up (as explained in the previous section). You should now be facing up hill, standing with your toe edge dug into the snow, your board perpendicular to the fall line and your weight distributed equally over both feet.

To begin your sideslip, gradually release the toe edge pressure and flatten the board toward the snow but without applying any pressure to the heel edge. Release some of the bend in your ankles and knees, not all of it. If you apply pressure to your heels, your downhill edge will catch, and Kablam! You are down on your back. When you have released enough pressure on the toe edge, your board will begin to slide sideways down the hill. You are sideslipping! Keep the board perpendicular to the fall line, and reapply pressure to the toe edge to slow down and apply even more pressure to stop.

Sideslipping will help you figure out how much pressure you have to apply to your edge to get your board to slow down and stop smoothly. Practice toe-side sideslipping very slowly, and then with a little more speed. Your motion should be fluid. If your motion is jerky and unbalanced, it will show in your tracks, which will be slashed with edge marks and most likely be punctuated with sitz marks! (When you "sitz" down on the snow, you leave a print called a sitz mark.)

After you get the hang of toeside sideslipping, let's try heelside. Start with your body facing downhill and the board perpendicular to the fall line. Your heel edge is pressured and dug into the snow. To start sideslipping, release some of the heel edge pressure but without letting your toe edge catch in the snow. Use the backs of your boots and bindings for leg support. Your knees really need to bend. Keep your arms in front of you for balance. Release heel pressure until the board is almost flat on the snow. Watch out for your toe edge! If you apply any pressure to your toes, you'll catch that edge and slam face first into the snow (a maneuver commonly referred to as the "body slam").

Practice sideslipping until you can make a smooth track on both toe and heel edges and you can speed up, slow down or stop exactly where you want to. Once you are proficient at sideslipping, you have found your edges.

UPHILL
DOWNHILL

START
HERE

PRESSURE
AND RELEASE
TOE EDGE

YOUR
SIDESLIP
TRACKS

FALL LINE

KEEP HEEL EDGE LIFTED

DIRECTION OF TRAVEL
IS ALONG THE
FALL LINE

FIG. 51: TOE-SIDE SIDESLIP

UPHILL
DOWNHILL

YOUR HEELSIDE
SIDESLIP
TRACK

PRESSURE AND RELEASE
HEEL EDGE

KEEP TOE EDGE CLEAR OF
THE SNOW

FIG. 52: HEEL-SIDE SIDESLIP

TURNING: Okay, now that you've found your edges, you can begin making some TURNS. Let's start by thinking about weight and pressure. Consider your foot and how you can vary your weight distribution on it (fig. 53). If you apply weight or pressure to the center or arch of your foot, you will cause your board to ride flat on the snow. If you apply pressure to your toe or heel, you will be riding the respective edge of your board. Here's the rule for learning to turn: You will want your board to ride flat on the snow when it is pointed straight down the fall line, and you will want to be pressuring an edge when you are either turning toward or away from straight down the fall line.

Positioning your CM correctly over the board is crucial when you are turning. Remember that the weighted end of the board goes down the hill first. That's why to glide straight down the hill you slide your hips forward until approximately 75 percent of your weight is over your front leg (fig. 54). However, as you make turns, you'll have to reposition your body in relation to the board. When traveling across the hill (perpendicular to the fall line), you'll have to shift your weight until it is evenly distributed over both legs (fig. 55), just as you did for sideslipping. Then, as you begin to turn downhill,

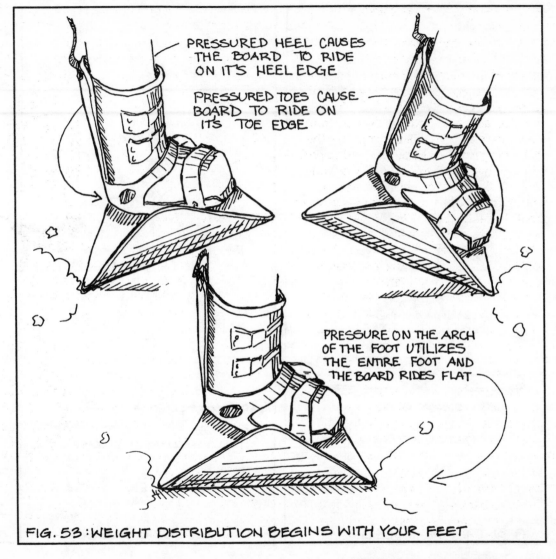

PRESSURED HEEL CAUSES THE BOARD TO RIDE ON ITS HEEL EDGE

PRESSURED TOES CAUSE BOARD TO RIDE ON ITS TOE EDGE

PRESSURE ON THE ARCH OF THE FOOT UTILIZES THE ENTIRE FOOT AND THE BOARD RIDES FLAT

FIG. 53: WEIGHT DISTRIBUTION BEGINS WITH YOUR FEET

you'll begin to shift your weight forward again.

By shifting the position of your hips, you can keep your CM in the right place. Remember, hips forward when you're headed down the hill and hips centered over both feet when you're headed across the hill. To demonstrate the importance of this concept, try the following from a stopped, standing position: Shove your hips toward the front of your board, over your forward foot. Now, shift them back toward your back foot. What happened to the pressure on the bottom of your lead foot? It shifted way back with you hips! If your hips drift back or side to side, so will your weight, then Kablam!

Now let's make a hypothetical turn using edge pressure and weight distribution. Imagine yourself starting down the fall line in a straight glide; 75 percent of your weight is over your front foot. You are pressuring the arch or center of your foot and your board is flat on the snow. To initiate the turn, pivot the board beneath you by gently kicking back with your back foot. At the same time, smoothly shift your weight toward the toe edge of your board and begin to pressure the toe edge. When you do this, the back end of your board will pivot and you will cross the fall line with the pressured edge. As your turn

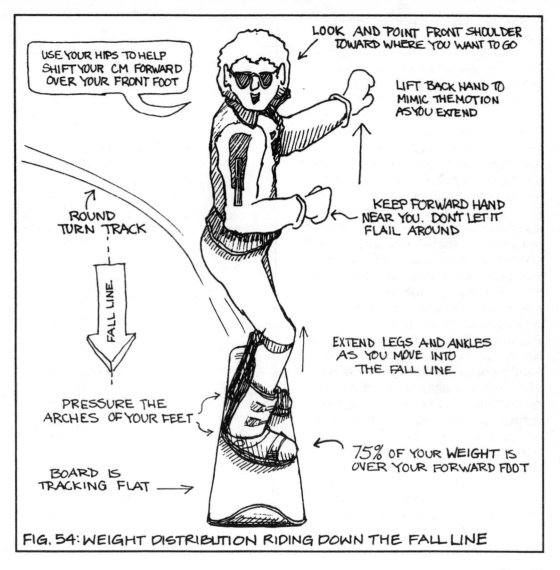

FIG. 54: WEIGHT DISTRIBUTION RIDING DOWN THE FALL LINE

continues, you will be approaching a path of travel perpendicular to the fall line. While this is happening, slowly shift your weight from your front foot to centered over both feet.

There are two more motions you must incorporate to make a smooth turn. They are flexion and extension. This is when snowboarding gets like patting your head and rubbing your stomach at the same time. You must concentrate. Your whole body, and especially your legs, should extend into a graceful, standing position as you ride down the fall line. Don't extend so far as to straighten or lock your knees but let your body sort of float up into an effortless, extended position. As you begin to turn away from the fall line, you'll want to begin to flex down until, when you're riding perpendicular to the fall line, you're in a slightly crouched, compacted position. Your flex and extend motion should be graceful and patient. Avoid bending at the waist or sudden, jerky movements. Exaggerate the motion at first, until you automatically flex down into the turn and extend up into the fall line.

With a bit of practice, the subtle shifts of weight and pressure and the flexing and extending will become natural and easy; but for now you must concentrate on where you want your

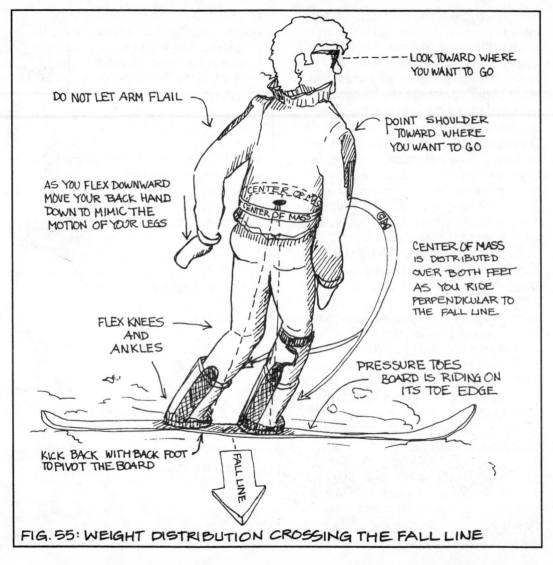

LOOK TOWARD WHERE YOU WANT TO GO

DO NOT LET ARM FLAIL

POINT SHOULDER TOWARD WHERE YOU WANT TO GO

AS YOU FLEX DOWNWARD MOVE YOUR BACK HAND DOWN TO MIMIC THE MOTION OF YOUR LEGS

CENTER OF MASS

CENTER OF MASS

CENTER OF MASS IS DISTRIBUTED OVER BOTH FEET AS YOU RIDE PERPENDICULAR TO THE FALL LINE

FLEX KNEES AND ANKLES

PRESSURE TOES BOARD IS RIDING ON ITS TOE EDGE

KICK BACK WITH BACK FOOT TO PIVOT THE BOARD

FALL LINE

FIG. 55: WEIGHT DISTRIBUTION CROSSING THE FALL LINE

Zen and the Art of Snowboarding

weight and remind yourself to flex and extend every time you make a turn. There's a lot to making a good turn, isn't there? Make sure to run through the steps in your mind before you get out on the hill (fig. 56). Then you'll need to go out and practice by making about a zillion turns. By then you should be looking pretty cool.

FIG. 56: VISUALIZE A PROPER TURN

TOESIDE TURN (figs. 57-58): Okay, enough with the hypothetical. Let's try a real turn. We'll start with the toeside turn. It's usually easier to learn than the heelside turn. A toeside turn is a turn to the left for goofy-foot boarders and to the right for regular footers. It's called a toeside turn because you finish the turn by facing up hill with pressure on the uphill edge of your board, which is where your toes are.

To make a toeside turn, start down the fall line in a straight glide. Your weight is over your front foot and you are pressuring your entire foot. The board is flat on the snow and your legs are extended. Point your front shoulder toward the direction you want to turn, and kick your back foot out as if you were kicking a ball behind you. Remember practicing static pivots? This is what they are for.

Concentrate on your weight placement and body movements as you begin to turn. Bend your knees and flex down as you drop in to the turn. Keep your back straight. After the board has pivoted, gradually shift the pressure from the center of your feet to your toes (your uphill edge). Your heel edge (your downhill edge) may lift slightly off the snow as your toe edge digs in. Shift your CM from your front foot to centered over both feet as you cross and ride perpendicular to the fall line. You are pressuring your toe edge and your legs are flexed. You have made a toeside turn!

To come to a stop, hold that body position (flexed), steer the tip of the board slightly uphill and increase the toe edge pressure, just as you did during the sideslipping exercise.

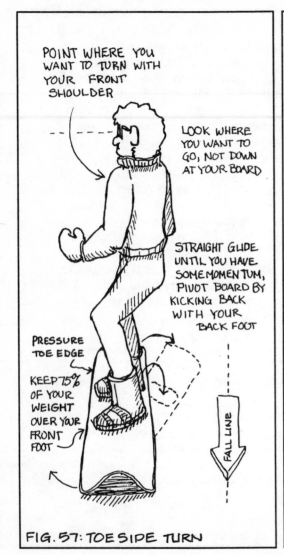

POINT WHERE YOU WANT TO TURN WITH YOUR FRONT SHOULDER

LOOK WHERE YOU WANT TO GO, NOT DOWN AT YOUR BOARD

STRAIGHT GLIDE UNTIL YOU HAVE SOME MOMENTUM, PIVOT BOARD BY KICKING BACK WITH YOUR BACK FOOT

PRESSURE TOE EDGE

KEEP 75% OF YOUR WEIGHT OVER YOUR FRONT FOOT

FALL LINE

FIG. 57: TOE SIDE TURN

START HERE

KEEP YOUR HANDS IN FRONT OF YOU

UPHILL DOWNHILL

FALL LINE

AFTER YOU CROSS THE FALL LINE, DIG IN WITH TOE EDGE TO STOP

STOP HERE

LIFT HEELS TO RELEASE HEEL EDGE

FIG. 58: FINISHING A TOESIDE TURN

HEELSIDE TURN (figs. 59-60): Okay, you've got it now! One more important maneuver to master, the heelside turn, and you are ready to go up the hill in the chair lift. In the heelside turn your backside will end up facing uphill. For goofys this is a turn to the right, a turn to the left for regulars.

To make a heelside turn, start down the hill in a straight glide right down the fall line with your legs extended and your weight over your front foot. Pressure the arch (center) of your foot to keep your board riding flat on the snow as you pick up momentum to initiate your turn. Lead with your front shoulder. It should point in the direction you intend to turn.

As in the toeside turn, you must concentrate on weight placement and body movement as you make your turn. Pivot the back of the board by kicking your back foot forward, as if kicking a ball. Begin the graceful downward motion by flexing your legs as you gradually apply edge pressure on the heel edge (your uphill edge) of your board. Your toe edge may lift off the snow slightly as your heel edge digs in. Keep your back straight as you shift your CM from your front foot to centered over both feet as you cross and ride perpendicular to the fall line. You have made a heelside turn! To come to a stop, hold that flexed position, steer the tip of your board slightly uphill and increase the heel edge pressure as you did in the heelside sideslip.

Practice making great big smooth round turns on your bunny hill until you can turn in both directions and can stop confidently. You must be able to control your speed and stop BEFORE you ride a lift. Practice! Once you have mastered turns and stops, you are ready to go further up the mountain. You are probably exhausted by now too and may want to call it a day. If so, find a hot tub, rest up, have a good dinner and hit the slopes relaxed and refreshed in the morning.

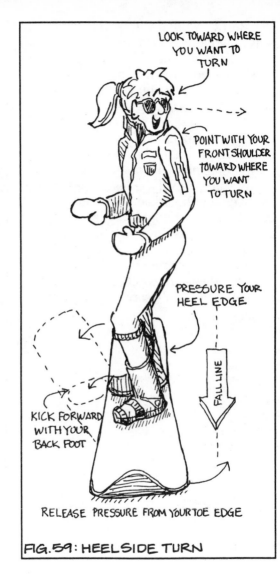

FIG. 59: HEELSIDE TURN

FIG. 60: FINISHING A HEELSIDE TURN

BASIC MANEUVERS (UNINTENDED):

While you're learning to snowboard, you will be performing all sorts of acrobatics that end up in sudden stops. I'll explain the most common boo-boos and how to avoid them. You will still slip, slide, crash and roll while you're learning. But at least you'll know what you're doing wrong and be able to correct your beginner's problems before they become chronic bad habits.

FACE CHRISTY OR FACE PLANT (fig. 61): If you do any or all of the following in the toeside turn, you'll probably catch your toe edge and end up very suddenly face down in the snow. OOf! 1. Break (bend) at the waist. 2. Let your body lean too far away from the board toward the hill. 3. Forget to bend your legs. 4. Pressure your edge too much or too suddenly. 5. Panic. To avoid the compromising position of a face plant, you must keep your CM over your board. Apply the pressure and weight shifts gradually and smoothly, and keep those knees and ankles flexing, not your waist.

THE BUTT DROP (fig. 62): This happens on your heelside turn if you lean too far back into the hill, your legs haven't flexed properly, your CM isn't over your board or you've tried to pressure your heel edge too suddenly. Ka-blam! The butt drop. You have created another fine sitz mark.

To keep the bunny hill free of sitz marks, remember all your motions and weight shifts. Flex those legs. Keep your CM over your board and use your arms for balance. Your board should be kept as flat on the snow as you can keep it, with just enough edge pressure to make the turn. Remember, shift your weight and edge pressure smoothly and gradually, and you'll stay up on your feet.

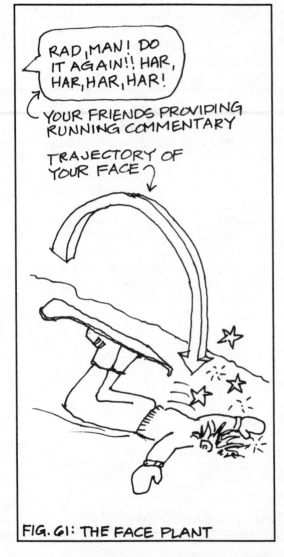

FIG. 61: THE FACE PLANT

FIG. 62: BASIC MANEUVERS (UNINTENDED): THE BUTT DROP

FIG. 63: BASIC MANEUVERS (UNINTENDED): THE SPINAL TAP

THE SPINAL TAP (fig. 63): This exciting fall is one you'll never forget. It's like doing a downhill butt drop but with a sumo wrestler adding a little shove.

It happens as you're making a transition from a toeside turn to a heelside turn. While on a toeside turn you begin to release the pressure from your toe edge to set up for your heelside turn. But yikes, too much pressure too soon to your heel edge and you snag that downhill (heel) edge. POW! You slam back first to the ground with your body downhill from your board. Ouch! Close your eyes and relax for a few seconds before you try to get up.

To avoid spinal taps, be patient when shifting from toe edge to heel edge. Let the board travel flat until you've crossed the fall line, then carefully apply the edge pressure to your heels. Keep your legs bent, weight over the front foot, back straight and your head up.

ALL RIGHT! YOU'VE MASTERED THE BASIC MOVES AND YOU'RE READY TO GO UP THE MOUNTAIN. WELCOME TO THE WORLD OF LIFTS.

A LITTLE ZEN ON LIFTS IN GENERAL:

Now that you're able to do all your maneuvers on your carefully chosen bunny hill, you'll want to try them on a bigger hill. Unless you're really into spending all day sidestepping up that hill, you'll have to learn how to ride a lift.

Before you attempt to get on a lift, there are a few things you should know. First, there are several different kinds of lifts. All are perpetual motion machines designed to carry, push or pull you up the hill. Some are easy to use and some require more skill and strength.

The lift line is another thing that you need to be warned about. When you try to approach your first lift, you will most likely encounter a mob of people between you and it. This bantering crowd is commonly known as the lift line. You will have to take your place, and spend anywhere from 45 seconds to 45 minutes waiting and weaving your way through a maze of ropes, poles and people while you politely answer silly questions about snowboarding. You will then encounter the ticket checker and finally the loading area.

You will spend a lot of time in lift lines and on lift rides, sometimes a lot longer than you'd like. Have patience, don't cut in line, keep your sense of humor, and these times will be good ones. If you encounter an unusually long lift line, consider riding another lift or look for a singles lane along the outside of the general maze. Singles lanes are areas where people skiing without partners can pair up for the lift ride. Generally they move more quickly than other lines. If you do have to get in a long line, make the most of it. Meet a handsome stranger in stretch pants, and learn some new jokes. Lift lines can be fun.

Lift attendants are very helpful and important people, particularly when you are learning to ride lifts. They run the whole program, and if you tick them off, they can trip you up. If it's your first lift ride, let the attendant know so he or she can assist you.

Ask if he or she will slow it down while you're loading. They are usually more than agreeable to this request. If they don't get you on the lift right the first time, their work has quadrupled since when you fall they have to stop the lift, pick you up, pick up your gear that you dropped, pick up whoever has by now crashed into you and their gear, then drag everyone and all the gear back to the lift, get everyone situated properly on the chair, call the attendant at the top to give the "all clear" signal and THEN start the lift back up. Falling off lifts is not the recommended way to make new friends at a ski resort, but it's a guaranteed way to get lots of people to notice you!

In the event you do fall while getting on or off the lift, don't feel alone. Almost every beginner to ever ride a lift has fallen at least once. The lower-mountain lift attendants are used to beginners and their boo-boos.

But you can't just count on the lift attendants to save you if you fall. You have to look out for yourself also. Remember that when you fall, the lift will continue to drag people and equipment over you until the operator manages to intervene. If you fall on a chair lift, DUCK! If the operator doesn't turn off the lift in time, the next chair and/or rider could hit you. If you fall on a surface lift, get out of the way of oncoming skiers. Whenever you fall, listen for the lift attendants' orders and follow them quickly.

Once you get on a lift, don't panic if it slows or stops. It almost invariably means that someone has fallen getting on or off the lift and the attendants have stopped to clean up the mess. Stay where you are. If you are in a chair lift, under no circumstances should you jump even if it looks like only a few feet to the ground. You could easily injure yourself or derail the chair and endanger everyone on it. No matter how long the ride takes, it's better to arrive cold and safe to the top than to be delivered to the bottom in a ski patrol basket.

Remember that mountain lifts are man-made machines with no brains. Once you walk over and take a look at the operation, you've outsmarted it. Always familiarize yourself visually with the loading process before you get in the lift line. Watch how the people are getting on the lift, then visualize yourself going through the motions of loading and unloading.

FIG. 65: BE PREPARED TO SPEND A LOT OF TIME IN LIFT LINES

FIG. 66: TAKE YOUR FIRST RIDE ON A CHAIR LIFT WITH AN EXPERIENCED PERSON. TRY TO STAY CALM.

CHAIR LIFTS:

As a beginner snowboarder, chair lifts will be the easiest type of lift for you to learn to ride, and they allow you to rest and take in the scenery while you're riding up. The first thing you should do is look for the loading area marks and watch the loading procedure. Look at your trail map to find out where this lift will drop you off. If it lets you off at a black diamond run called "So Long Sucker!" this is the wrong lift. Check your map for an easier one, "Simple Simon" or "Easy Street," marked with a green circle.

Once you've determined that this is the right lift and have an idea how to get on, partner up. Most chair lifts carry two people per chair; some carry three or more. Partner up according to how many people the chair accommodates. If you don't have a partner, find the singles lane. If there is no singles lane, call out "single!" and someone that is also looking for a partner will wave you over. The singles game is, incidentally, the only acceptable way for you to cut into the line. Sometimes the lift operator will send you to the front of the line to partner up with someone, and it's a great way to meet people.

Try to take your first lift ride with experienced riders. They'll coach you through your first attempt. If you're riding with another snowboarder, try to get someone with the opposite stance. Put goofy foot on the right side and regular foot on the left. This way you will be facing away from each other and won't collide when you get off the chair.

Okay, you've got a partner, your back foot is out of the binding, let's go! Skate through the maze without running over the tails of anyone else's skies or boards and stay with your partner. When the attendant tells you to, move all the way into the indicated loading area with your board pointing straight ahead (fig. 67), in the direction the chair is traveling. Look back over your shoulder for the vertical bar of the approaching chair, or the side rail, reach back toward it and wait until the chair touches the back of your knee. Now, here comes the tricky part; sit down! You did it! You are in the chair. Keep your tip up and pointed straight ahead. If there is a retention bar, alert your partner(s), then reach overhead, grasp the bar and slowly lower it into place in front of you.

There are a few things you should pay attention to as you are riding the chair. First, keep your board pointed straight ahead (up hill in the direction of travel). This is very important, particularly when you pass lift towers. Some towers are situated close enough to the chairs that if your board is sideways, it can snag on them and pitch you right out of your seat! Second, sit still. Don't rock or bounce the chair. It could derail the cable, which is potentially very dangerous. Another thing that happens when you ride chairs is that your board will feel heavy dangling from your lead foot. To alleviate the pull on your front ankle, support the board with the toe of your free back foot by slipping it under the heel edge of your board.

After a few minutes (how few depends on how high you are going and how many times the lift stops for falling people), you will approach the top and must prepare to unload (fig. 68). There are usually signs on the loft towers indicating this. They might say "raise retention bar" or "prepare to unload" or "keep your tips up." You should do all these things, and make sure that you, your partner, your clothing or equipment is not snagged on the chair or each other. Your gloves should be on your hands, with your hands on the front of the seat.

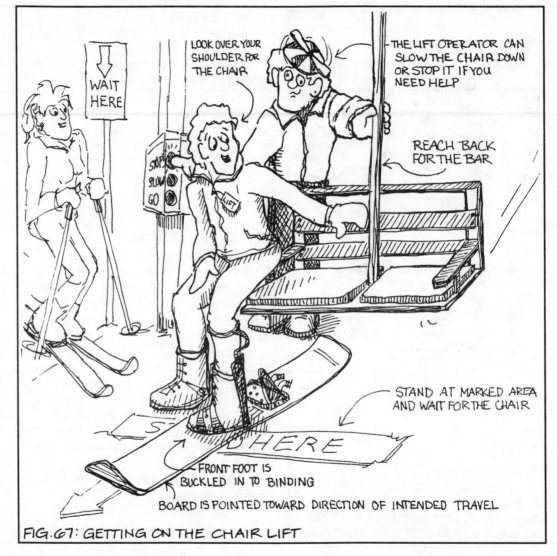

FIG. 67: GETTING ON THE CHAIR LIFT

To unload, keep your board pointed straight ahead with your back foot resting on the nonskid pad. Resist the urge to leap out of the chair early. Let the unloading ramp rise up or the chair drop down until your board touches the snow. There will be a sign that says "Stand up HERE." Do exactly that exactly there! Lean forward, push off the chair with your hands and stand up at the indicated mark. Keep your weight forward and glide down the ramp. It won't be very steep, in fact it may be so gentle that you may have to skate to get completely away from the unloading area promptly. Find a safe place on the side of the trail well out of the ramp traffic, and buckle in your back foot.

If for some reason you miss all the signs, forget what to do, panic or fall asleep on the chair, you will go right past the unloading ramp. If this happens, don't jump! Your chair will travel a short distance until your board strikes a wand, which stops the chair or alerts the operator. Stay seated and wait for instructions. There is usually a second (secret) ramp for employee and VIP unloading, which you will use. The main hazard of unloading in this manner is a busted ego. An alarm may ring, everyone will stop and look and most likely point and whistle to make sure no one misses the dork-on-the-chair spectacle.

FIG. 68: GETTING OFF THE CHAIRLIFT LIKE A PRO

SURFACE LIFTS:

Surface lifts are lifts that drag you along the surface of the snow rather than carry you over it. You'll find surface lifts a lot more difficult to use than chair lifts. If you have a choice, use the chair lifts until you are fairly adept at steering your board. If you must start out with surface lifts, try to find a rope tow. It is the simplest of the surface lifts to load and unload from.

ROPE TOW (fig. 69): A rope tow is a continuous loop of heavy rope or cable which turns on sheaves, one at the top of the mountain and one at the bottom. Go through the lift line just as you would for the chair lift, but there's no need to get a partner—you're on your own. Stand on the loading mark next to the rope. Point your board uphill, in the direction of travel. Your back foot should be free and placed on the non-skid pad. When you're ready, put your hands around the rope and slowly tighten your grip. Keep your back straight, legs flexed, and lean back a little with some weight over your back foot. As you start to move, keep your board heading straight up the hill and in the groove made by the previous tow traffic.

LET THE ROPE SLIP THROUGH YOUR FINGERS UNTIL YOU ARE BALANCED, THEN GRIP SLOWLY

ALWAYS WEAR HEAVY GLOVES ON A ROPE TOW

STEER THE BOARD STRAIGHT AND STAY IN THE TRACK

FRONT FOOT IS BUCKLED IN BINDING

BACK FOOT IS RESTING ON THE NON-SKID PAD

ZOOM

FIG. 69: SURFACE LIFTS: THE ROPE TOW

If you lose control, you can just step off with your back foot to help reposition your board, or let go of the rope and get out of the way. If you let go or fall, watch out for the people coming behind you. This lift may not stop if you fall, so get out of the way quickly.

When you get to the top, just let go and skate out of the unloading area. Move to the edge of the trail, out of the traffic flow and then buckle in your back foot.

T-BAR LIFTS (fig. 70): T-bars are more complicated to get positioned on and require (as do all surface lifts) strength and balance. It also helps, but is not required, to have a partner. Your best partner will be an experienced T-bar rider. He can direct you and demonstrate proper technique. With your back foot free, move up to the loading area, facing your partner with your board pointed uphill. The lift attendant will hand you the T-bar from behind. Place the cross bar behind your butt. REMAIN STANDING! DO NOT TRY TO SIT DOWN ON THE T-BAR! The T-bar is spring-loaded and will drop to the ground with you if you sit down on it. Hold onto the center bar with both hands and keep your back straight and your legs flexed. Lean back slightly and keep your board gliding straight. Don't

FIG. 70: SURFACE LIFTS: THE T-BAR

let it turn and move across the track. Use your back foot to steer.

Before you reach the top, determine who will be the one to release the T-bar. Let's say it's you this time. When you reach the designated unloading area at the top, your partner will remove himself from the T-bar and glide away. You (the one to release the bar) will then remove the bar from your thigh, pull it back and then around in front of you. Let it go carefully at the sign that says "unload here." Make sure there are no skiers or boarders in the path of the T-bar before you let it go. Remember, it's spring-loaded and will snap up to the overhead cable. Anything in its path will get snapped, snagged, pummeled and probably hurt.

Once you've released the T-bar, move quickly out of the unloading area. After you see those T-bars zzzzzing to the overhead cable, you won't hesitate to clear the unloading area. Move to the side of the trail and then buckle in your back foot. You are shred ready.

THE DISC LIFT:
Disc lifts are very similar to T-bar lifts. They require the same finesse at the loading ramp and strength and balance on the ride up. The main difference is the disc lift carries only one person, while the T-bar can carry one or two people. The disc lift, or Poma (Poma is a brand name which is widely used to refer to any disc-type lift), is a bar with a round plastic or metal disc at the end of it suspended from a continuous-loop overhead cable.

This is what you have to do to get on the Poma (fig. 71): With your back foot unbuckled, begin by approaching the loading area alone. Stop in the loading area with your board pointed directly uphill, your eventual direction of travel. The lift operator will hand you the disc from the front. Lift your free foot and place the bar between your legs, with the disc behind you. The disc will rest against your butt and upper thighs. The bar will protrude from between your legs, out in front of you. This bar is what you hold onto. The Poma does not stop for you to load, so be ready to glide as soon as the lift operator hands you the disc.

You will be tempted to sit down on the disc, but don't. It's spring-loaded like the T-bar. If you sit down, the disc will drop to the ground and dump you. Keep your back straight, legs flexed, back foot resting on the nonskid pad and lean slightly back, putting weight on your back foot. Keep your tip pointed in the direction of travel, and don't let your board get out of the groove. Stay centered over your board. If you do all of these things, you won't fall.

If you blow it and fall, you will most likely be tangled up and snagged on the disc and get dragged up the hill. This is not particularly dangerous, but it is rather humiliating. To detach yourself from the Poma, simply pull the disc from between your legs, hold it away from your body and let it go. Then move out of the track quickly so you don't take anyone down with you or get run over.

Assuming you reach the top, unload as you did from the T-bar. Pull the disc back, lift up your free foot and move the disc around in front of and away from your body. Make sure the unloading area is clear, then let go of it gently. Move away from the unloading area immediately. The disc zzzzings up to the overhead cable just as the T-bar did, and you don't want one to hit you. When you are a safe distance away and on the side of the trail, buckle in.

BASIC MANEUVERS (UNINTENDED): THE DOG PILE (fig. 72):

Riding lifts doesn't always go as smoothly as you'd like. It's common for beginner lift riders to fall, both when loading and especially when unloading a lift.

Unfortunately, even a small, innocent fall can quickly turn into a semi-apocalyptic event called a "dog pile." It all happens very quickly—one guy falls and he usually drags his partner(s) down with him. When the people in the next chair see the chaos, they panic. They proceed to fall all over one another and crash into others already down on the ramp, then the next chair, etc. The dog pile will hopelessly multiply until the lift operator hits the stop button. He will then attempt to extricate the entangled

GRIP THE BAR FIRMLY WITH BOTH HANDS

BACK IS STRAIGHT

KEEP THE BOARD IN THE TRACK

KNEES ARE FLEXED

LEAN AGAINST THE DISK, DON'T SIT DOWN!

FRONT FOOT IS BUCKLED IN

GUIDE THE BOARD IN THE TRACK WITH THE FREE BACK FOOT, THEN REST IT ON THE NON-SKID

FIG. 71: RIDING THE DISC LIFT

people and equipment from one another and get them up and away from the ramp and reunited with their ski poles, goggles, hats and other gear. The event may be accompanied by shouts, whistles, jostling, groping and shoving.

Overall, a dog pile is an unpleasant experience, so avoid starting one by getting off the lift correctly the first time. Be prepared to unload when you reach the top of the ramp. Stand up at the indicated time and place. Keep most of your weight over your front foot when you get off the lift and glide straight to the end of the ramp, then immediately move away from the unloading area. If you do fall, watch your head (duck) and move out of the way quickly before you become the bottom of the pile.

If there is already a dog pile on the ramp in front of you, look for an escape route. There is usually enough room on the ramp to make a turn around the pile. If there isn't enough room to turn, you can stop by putting your back foot down and then skate around the scene. Try to do this without knocking your partner over. If you have your turns and straight glides down pat before going up the lift, you'll be able to avoid existing dog piles and prevent starting one of your own.

FIG. 72: THE DOG PILE

Zen and the Art of Snowboarding

ELEMENTS OF TURNING:

Okay, let's assume you've made it to the top of the run on a lift. You are buckled in and shred ready, but gee, that looks steep! There's a nice, easy, wide-open area down there, but getting to it looks impossible. Well, it's not really all that steep; but when you arrive at the top of new terrain, it will often appear steeper and more narrow and treacherous than it really is. Don't let the hill psych you out! You can do it. Remember the sideslip? You can get down just about anything by doing the sideslip. Go right down the fall line doing a toeside sideslip to get down the scary part and out to that nice easy part of the run.

Another thing that may intimidate you on the mountain is getting too close to the edge of the trail. It's generally not as dangerous as you imagine it to be, but it is difficult to concentrate on your maneuvers if you are overwhelmed with a feeling of impending doom. Again, don't let the terrain psych you out. Beginner slopes rarely have bottomless crevices or rocky cliffs lurking just beyond their boundaries. You already know how to stop, and I'll explain a simple way to maneuver sideways. With these skills, you will feel more confident near the edge.

FIG. 73: YOU MAY HAVE TO SIDESLIP OR TRAVERSE DOWN TO AN EASIER PART OF THE RUN

If you get too close to the side of the trail, you can traverse, which simply means to travel across the run. When you traverse, you move slightly down hill and mainly across the terrain. You can go either right or left, tip first (forward) or tail first (backward). You traverse the direction you want to go on your toe or heel edge.

Let's start with a toeside traverse. You are standing facing up the hill, with your board perpendicular to the fall line and your toe edge (your uphill edge) dug in. Your weight is distributed over both feet. To traverse across the hill to your right, look and point your right shoulder to the right. Keep your board across the fall line, and gradually release some of the pressure from your uphill edge. Point the correct part of your board (tip for goofy, tail for regular) slightly downhill in the direction you want to go by slightly shifting some weight (not very much, or you'll go downhill instead of across) to your lead foot. You will slip/skid across the hill and slightly downhill.

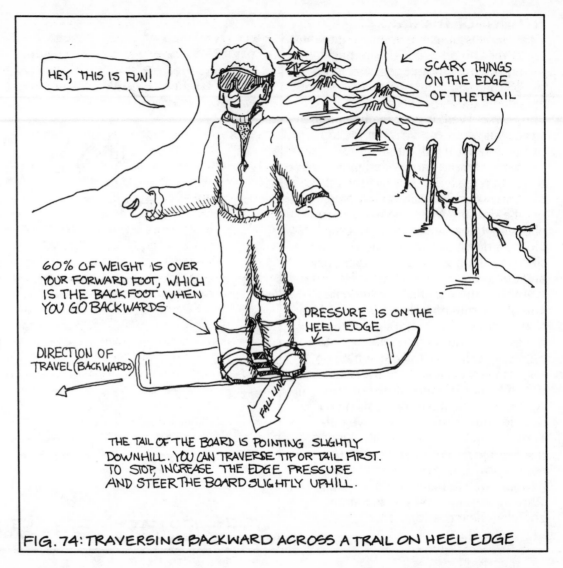

FIG. 74: TRAVERSING BACKWARD ACROSS A TRAIL ON HEEL EDGE

Zen and the Art of Snowboarding

If you are picking up too much speed, you are probably pointing your board downhill too much. This is generally caused by too much weight over the lead foot. Correct your stance, steer across the hill and apply more edge pressure to slow down. When you've traversed to where you want to be, steer your board slightly uphill, and apply more toe edge pressure to stop.

To toeside traverse to the left, repeat the process in the opposite direction. This time you'll be going backward to the left if you were going forward to the right, and forward if you were going backward. Release some of the pressure from your toeside (uphill) edge, and point you left shoulder to the left. Point your board (the tail if you're goofy and the tip if you're regular) down the hill a little. Come to a stop by steering the lead end of your board slightly uphill and adding more edge pressure.

You can traverse both forward and backward and on either heel or toe edge, whichever is your uphill edge. Once you learn to traverse on your toe edge, go ahead and try it on your heel edge. It's not really any more difficult than the toeside traverse, but it is scarier because you will be facing down the hill. Don't forget to watch where you are going! Since you can go forward and backward, skiers cannot anticipate your moves. It's your responsibility to avoid collisions. Contrary to popular opinion, staring down at your board does not improve steering or speed control. Practice does.

Now that you've sideslipped or traversed to a wide easy slope, let's get started improving your turning skills so that you can made a series of linked turns—toeside, then heelside, then toeside, etc. You already know how to make a sliding pivot (turn) in both directions, sideslip, traverse and stop. Let's combine these skills to learn garlands and linked sideslips, then we'll go on to the patience turn and linked skidded turns.

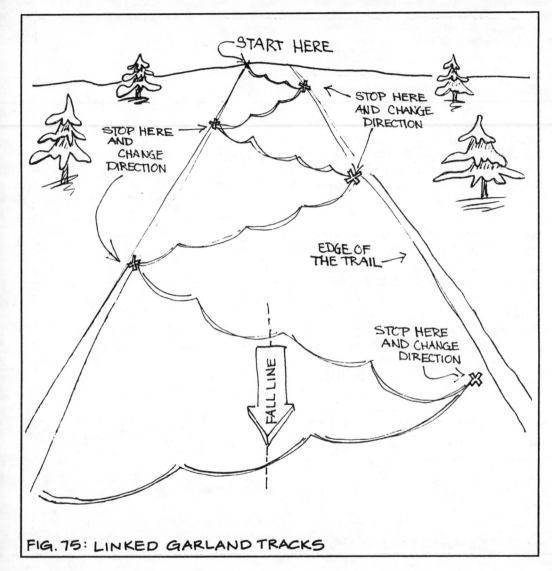

FIG. 75: LINKED GARLAND TRACKS

Labels in figure:
START HERE
STOP HERE AND CHANGE DIRECTION
STOP HERE AND CHANGE DIRECTION
EDGE OF THE TRAIL
STOP HERE AND CHANGE DIRECTION
FALL LINE

GARLANDS:

"What's a garland?" you ask. Well, imagine a garland on a Christmas tree. That's the shape your track should resemble (fig. 75). Garlands are a series of linked turns in one direction. Your direction of travel is mainly across the hill. Your change of direction is minimal, and you don't actually cross the fall line with the front of your board with each "turn" or link in your garland.

To make toeside garlands, start out in a straight glide and make a toeside turn. Before you come to a stop, release some of that toe edge pressure and extend your legs as you unweight. Shift your hips forward over your front foot, and let the tip of the board drift downhill toward, but not all the way into or across, the fall line. Your speed will increase. Once you have momentum, flex your legs and pivot in another toeside turn. Repeat this until you can do a series of toeside garlands without stopping. You should be flexing down into the turns and extending up as your tip drifts toward the fall line. When you reach the side of the trail (remember, your main direction of travel is across the hill) turn and do garlands on your heel side until you reach the opposite side of the trail. You should now be starting to get the feel of smooth, continuous, linked movements with flexion and extension in each one, and without stopping between "links."

LINKED SIDESLIPS:

Okay, now it's time to try some linked sideslipping. This is a maneuver where you sideslip on one edge, pivot and then sideslip on the other edge (fig. 76). First, start down the hill in a straight glide. You are standing tall, your board is flat on the snow and you are picking up speed. Pivot the board, and as you cross the fall line, flex down, pressure your uphill edge and sideslip. Once you have speed control and balance in your sideslip without stopping, extend your legs and unweight your edge as you stand up, shift your hips over your front foot and pivot the board in the other direction. Flex down, sideslip, extend up, pivot, etc. If you can link your sideslips with turns (pivots) and without stopping and can make garlands in both directions, you have mastered the edge pressure and weight shifts enough to make a patience turn and then go on to link some turns.

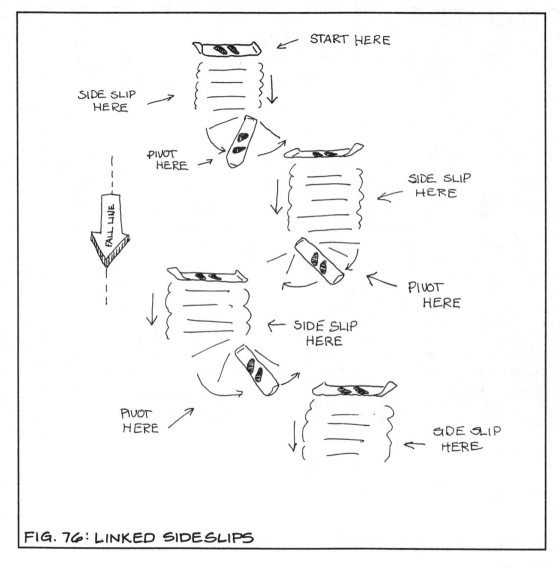

FIG. 76: LINKED SIDESLIPS

PATIENCE TURN:

To make a patience turn, you will rely primarily on weight placement (pressure control) to guide your board through the turn. This turn happens more slowly than the sliding pivot and the rudimentary toeside and heelside turns you've already practiced, hence the name "patience" turn. You will use a shift in your CM to initiate the turn and then very patiently hold the position until the board turns.

Since the patience turn will have you pointed down the fall line for quite a while, be sure to practice on a gentle slope– one on which you could comfortably glide straight down. Start off (fig. 77) in a traverse with your legs flexed and with equal weight on each foot. Using your hips, shift your weight back (over your back foot) until the board stalls to nearly a stop. Next, use your lead shoulder and your head to direct the turn by pointing them down the fall line. At the same time, make an exaggerated weight shift forward by moving your hips toward the tip of the board. As your hips move forward, extend your legs. The board will turn if you are smooth with your movement (and patient). After the board has turned 90 degrees and is turning through the fall line, shift your weight again to your

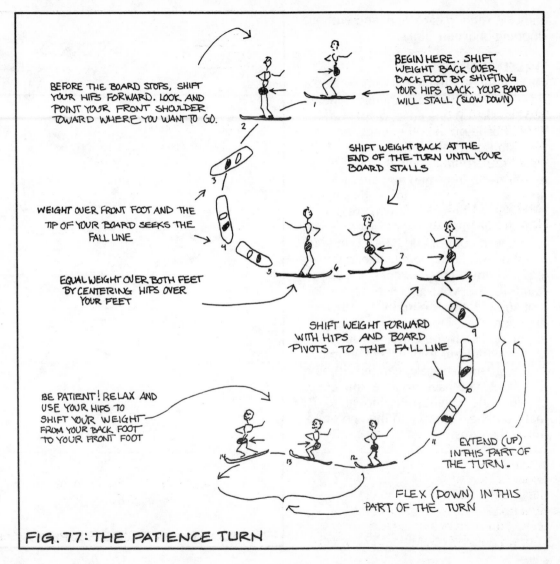

BEGIN HERE. SHIFT WEIGHT BACK OVER BACK FOOT BY SHIFTING YOUR HIPS BACK. YOUR BOARD WILL STALL (SLOW DOWN)

BEFORE THE BOARD STOPS, SHIFT YOUR HIPS FORWARD. LOOK AND POINT YOUR FRONT SHOULDER TOWARD WHERE YOU WANT TO GO.

SHIFT WEIGHT BACK AT THE END OF THE TURN UNTIL YOUR BOARD STALLS

WEIGHT OVER FRONT FOOT AND THE TIP OF YOUR BOARD SEEKS THE FALL LINE

EQUAL WEIGHT OVER BOTH FEET BY CENTERING HIPS OVER YOUR FEET

SHIFT WEIGHT FORWARD WITH HIPS AND BOARD PIVOTS TO THE FALL LINE

BE PATIENT! RELAX AND USE YOUR HIPS TO SHIFT YOUR WEIGHT FROM YOUR BACK FOOT TO YOUR FRONT FOOT

EXTEND (UP) IN THIS PART OF THE TURN.

FLEX (DOWN) IN THIS PART OF THE TURN

FIG. 77: THE PATIENCE TURN

Zen and the Art of Snowboarding

back foot until the board turns up onto a traverse and stalls.

The patience turn teaches you the fine points of controlling your CM in relation to the board. Remember that the predominant skill to practice with the patience turn is pressure control. Minimize your rotary (pivoting) motions. Patiently allow your weight shifts, flexing and extending to guide your board through the turn.

SKIDDED LINKED TURNS:

Now we can get on to some serious turning! In the skidded link turn you will travel a path that is mostly down the fall line. This exercise is very similar to linked sideslips, but you won't be sideslipping between turns, so you'll pick up more speed. As with the patience turn, practice on a slope that is gentle enough that you can glide straight down the fall line without giving yourself an anxiety attack.

Start down the fall line in a straight glide. Pivot the board across the fall line about 45 degrees (not very far) and flex down. Then extend up again, shift your weight over your front foot and let the tip go back into the fall line. Now pivot the board 45 degrees in the opposite direction, flex down, then shift your weight forward again, extend up, get your tip pointed down the fall line, pi-

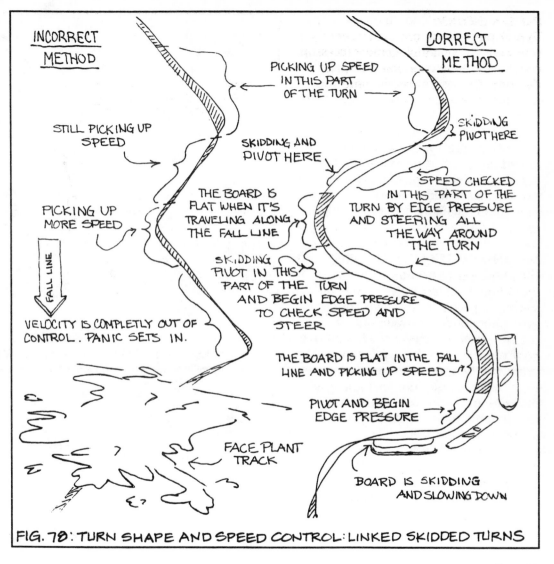

FIG. 78: TURN SHAPE AND SPEED CONTROL: LINKED SKIDDED TURNS

vot, flex down, extend up, pivot, etc. Repeat one million times.

Okay! You've really made some progress now. You've been practicing skidded linked turns for a while, and you are making a track down the fall line that is beginning to look like a continuous elongated "S" (fig. 78). Your speed is under control, and the motion of linked turns is starting to feel pretty good. Now let's refine these skills to make better linked turns so you can go on to more challenging terrain and ultimately look really cool.

MAKING BETTER LINKED TURNS (Beginning to look cool):

Right now your turns are rudimentary sliding, skidding rotary (pivot) motions. That's fine for easy terrain, but up on the steeper runs you'll need to improve your present skills, learn a few new ones and then practice and experiment to perfect your motion. Your goal is a series of graceful linked turns on any terrain, with total control of your turn shape, size and speed.

Let's start with two motions you've already been introduced to: flexing and extending. To achieve the grace and fluid motion of expert riders, you'll need

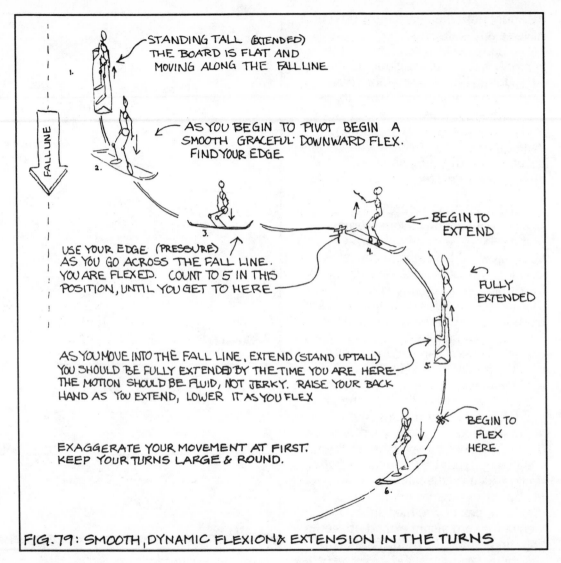

STANDING TALL (EXTENDED) THE BOARD IS FLAT AND MOVING ALONG THE FALL LINE

FALL LINE

AS YOU BEGIN TO PIVOT BEGIN A SMOOTH GRACEFUL DOWNWARD FLEX. FIND YOUR EDGE

BEGIN TO EXTEND

FULLY EXTENDED

USE YOUR EDGE (PRESSURE) AS YOU GO ACROSS THE FALL LINE. YOU ARE FLEXED. COUNT TO 5 IN THIS POSITION, UNTIL YOU GET TO HERE

AS YOU MOVE INTO THE FALL LINE, EXTEND (STAND UPTALL) YOU SHOULD BE FULLY EXTENDED BY THE TIME YOU ARE HERE. THE MOTION SHOULD BE FLUID, NOT JERKY. RAISE YOUR BACK HAND AS YOU EXTEND, LOWER IT AS YOU FLEX

BEGIN TO FLEX HERE.

EXAGGERATE YOUR MOVEMENT AT FIRST. KEEP YOUR TURNS LARGE & ROUND.

FIG. 79: SMOOTH, DYNAMIC FLEXION & EXTENSION IN THE TURNS

Zen and the Art of Snowboarding

to practice flexing and extending your knees and ankles during the entire turn. If you have a skiing background, applying this motion to the snowboard turn is probably already happening without much effort. If you do not ski, then you are probably flexing when you should be extending, extending when you should be flexing, forgetting to do either and/or crashing a lot.

You must flex and extend correctly if you want to get better. Correct flexing will make your weight distribution and edge pressure much more efficient and give you better control over your speed and steering. Your board will go where you want it to go, at the speed you intend it to travel. Graceful patient extending at the right time sets you up smoothly for your next turn, which is essential in executing continuous linked turns. Practice and perfect the skills of flexing and extending and you'll notice a big improvement in your snowboarding maneuvers.

To practice and perfect flexing and extending, begin on comfortable, easy terrain. Point your board down the fall line with your legs extended, standing tall. Begin a wide sweeping turn, using

FIG. 80: SETTLE SLOWLY, RISE GRADUALLY, PRACTICE FLEXING & EXTENDING

the entire width of the trail. As your board begins to pivot, start a slow and smooth downward flexing motion with your knees and ankles. Count to five slowly as you flex down and "settle" into the turn. Exaggerate the flexing motion.

As you reach the bottom or end of the turn and your board is perpendicular to the fall line, you should be flexed as low as you can go with your back straight. A common mistake in this part of the turn, however, is to break (bend) at the waist. To avoid breaking at the waist, concentrate on keeping your back straight as you flex down.

All right, you've flexed way down, now let's get back up, slowly. Begin a slow, smooth extending (standing) motion with your knees and ankles as the tip of your board moves toward the fall line. Count to five as you extend up. This motion unweights or releases the edge pressure and allows the board to gain the momentum you need to initiate the next turn. Your motion is fluid from extension to flexion. Don't bounce or suddenly jerk your legs and body to the desired position. Settle slowly, then gradually and gracefully rise up to the extended position as you unweight.

Use your back hand to help you get up and down gracefully, just as a ballet dancer would do. Mimic your body's up-and-down motion with your hand. Lift yourself up and out of the top of the turn by raising your back hand above shoulder level as you extend your legs, and as you settle into the bottom of the turn, drop your hand below waist level. The movement of your hand should be like the rest of your body motion: smooth, fluid and patient.

Practice flexing and extending by exaggerating the motion on wide, groomed, easy terrain until it becomes automatic. As you get better, the motion will become more subtle and increasingly graceful. It will begin to "feel right." By flexing, you have added efficiency to your edge pressure, and your extension sets you up for your next turn.

ECONOMY OF MOTION AND STANCE:

In addition to flexing and extending there are two other important components of turning you must work on to improve your form. They are economy of motion and stance.

Economy of motion is one of your most important considerations when you are trying to polish your snowboarding style. It's simply not possible to make elegant, smooth turns if your torso, hands and arms are flailing all over the place. Get rid of any upper body motion that is unnecessary. Keep your hands in front of your body if you find yourself swinging them around. Extra movement not only looks bad, but it causes shifts of weight which most likely will throw you off balance and cause you to fall, which also looks bad. Of course, the one area where economy of motion does not strictly apply is in the exaggerated flexing and extending we discussed previously. Just make sure your exaggerated movements are graceful and fluid, not jerky and sudden.

If you have good economy of motion and you are still having a difficult time smoothing out your turns, review your stance. Your posture should be controlled without being stiff. Your back should be straight without breaking at the waist. Keep your head up, and look and point your shoulder in the direction you intend to travel. Flex those knees and ankles and keep your weight where you want it. Your shoulders should be squared or parallel to the board. A good stance and economy of motion will keep you balanced over your board.

When you are working on improving your turns, it is often very difficult to accurately critique yourself. For this reason, it helps a lot to have an experienced rider watch you take a run or two and then tell you what you're doing wrong and how to improve.

SPEED CONTROL:

A very important skill, especially in steeper terrain, is speed control. A common beginner error is to pick up more and more speed on each successive turn. As your overall speed increases, so does your anxiety level, which will in most cases cause panic turns and crashes. The key to averting these problems is speed control. And the key to speed control is learning how to finish your turns.

If you're progressively picking up speed in successive turns, you are making a common mistake of trying to begin a new turn before you have completed the last one. You must get your speed under control by finishing one turn before you set up for the next one.

Slowing down (speed control) takes place mainly at the end or bottom of each turn. To achieve a proper finish at the bottom of a turn, start off on easy terrain and practice making large sweeping turns to give yourself plenty of time to think about what you are doing. As you go through the turn, spend more time flexing and settling into the turn. Count to five more slowly, exaggerate your flex more and increase your edge pressure. Be patient! Then smoothly extend back up and shift your weight forward. Let your board do some of the

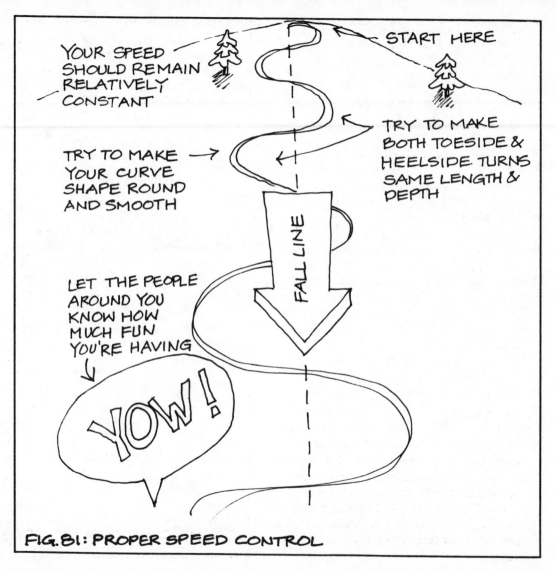

FIG. 81: PROPER SPEED CONTROL

work. Your forward weight shift will take the tip of your board back into the fall line with minimal pivoting motion from your back foot. Now you are set up for your next turn.

Another thing you should pay attention to is the shape of your turn. As you work on your turning skills, you should visualize smooth, rounded turns (fig. 81), and try to achieve the continuous "S" track in the snow, instead of the skidded track you would leave in the snow with your skidded, pivoting turns. Concentrate on keeping your arc the same size on your toeside turns as on your heelside turns. A well-rounded turn is generally a finished turn. Practice making large well-rounded linked turns until you are satisfied that your turn shape is correct and you have consistent speed control.

Once you have mastered all these skills in large slow turns, you can learn to make smaller turns. Since the turn radius is shorter, your moves must be done more quickly. This does not mean less gracefully. Do everything just like you did in a large turn, except make a slightly smaller turn radius each time. As you gradually shorten your turns, you will automatically begin to make the weight shifts, edge pressure changes and body motions more quickly. When

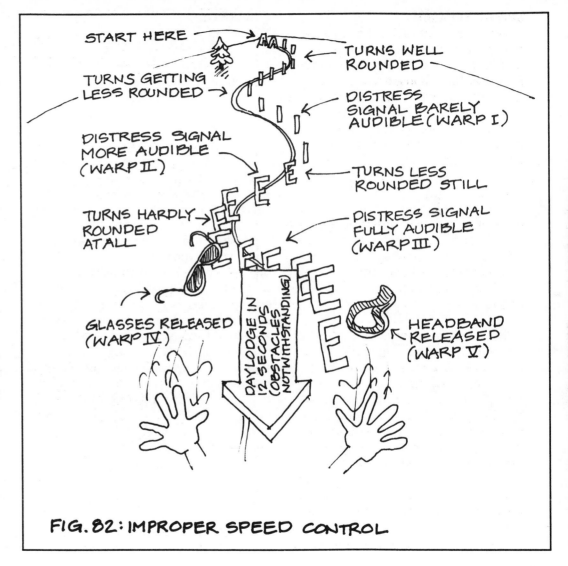

FIG. 82: IMPROPER SPEED CONTROL

making shorter radius turns, you will have a tendency to cut off the finishing part of your turn. You'll know you are falling into this deplorable but common habit if you find your speed increasing with each turn. To overcome this, review the skills for finishing a turn, and practice!

CARVING:

You've come a long way from that first sideslip to a skidded turn, and now you are ready to carve. Learning to carve your turns will really set you free. It's a matter of putting together all the techniques, skills and drills that you've learned so far, then taking it one step further, right to your edges.

So far you have learned that there are three basic ways your board interacts with the snow: slip (or glide), skid and carve. It can slip (or glide) on the snow without applying any edge, as in sideslipping or straight gliding. Skidding (what you're mostly doing now) happens when the board is sliding sideways or pivoting and you're applying some edge pressure to the snow. The board is very close to flat on the snow with just enough edge pressure to give some resistance. However, the board is still skidding over the snow instead of carving through it. As such, your skidded turns do not leave a distinct line or track in the snow. When you are carving your turns correctly, you'll be able to tell because your track through the snow will become defined and linear. Cool!

To transform your skidded turns into elegant carved turns, you will need a lot of practice, so let's get started with some exercises similar to the ones you already know, but with more emphasis on using your edges. Okay, take the lift up to the top of a nice easy run.

"Gee whiz! When do we get off this dumb bunny hill and onto something radical?" you ask. Well, as you practice new skills, you must concentrate only on the task at hand. If the terrain is terrifying, your concentration will be disrupted. So, learn the new skills on easy hills, build up your confidence, then go out to steeper terrain. When your ego needs boosting, go back to easier terrain.

Now, let's make some garlands again, but this time, concentrate on your edge pressure. Rather than making a skidded pivot in each garland, ride your edge more. The object is to get your rotary movement (the pivot) minimized and use your edge to ride through the turn. Practice large garlands in both directions (toe edge and heel edge) until you can ride through the link almost entirely on your edge. Keep each garland link large to give yourself plenty of time to experience the carving/edge feeling.

Next, do some traversing, but use your edges this time. When you traversed earlier, you were applying some edge pressure and slipping or skidding across the hill. Now as you traverse, increase your edge pressure to get up on your edge, and try not to slip or skid at all. Practice traversing until you can ride across the hill on both toe and heel edge without slipping and skidding.

Now that you have a feel for your edges, you can start making carved linked turns. Find a freshly groomed untracked run to check out the turns you're making (fig. 83). Make a few turns, stop and look back up the hill at your tracks. Do you see a distinct narrow track in the snow from one turn to the next, or did you leave a big skidded mess? If you are still sliding or skidding through the turns, try exaggerating the flex and extend motion and be more dynamic and powerful with your edge pressure.

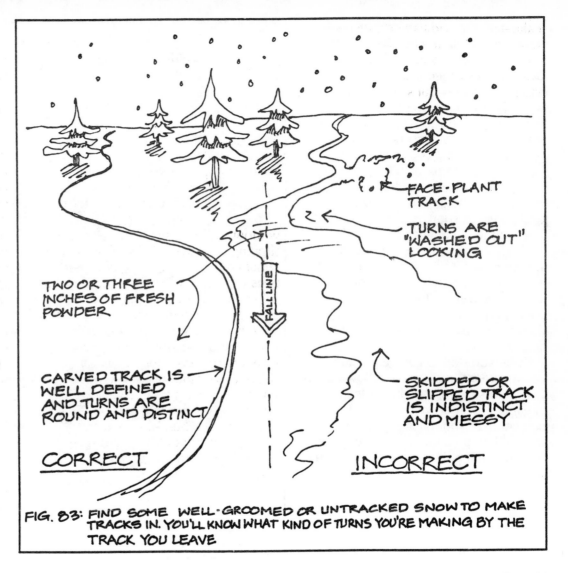

FACE-PLANT TRACK

TURNS ARE "WASHED OUT" LOOKING

TWO OR THREE INCHES OF FRESH POWDER

FALL LINE

CARVED TRACK IS WELL DEFINED AND TURNS ARE ROUND AND DISTINCT

SKIDDED OR SLIPPED TRACK IS INDISTINCT AND MESSY

CORRECT

INCORRECT

FIG. 83: FIND SOME WELL-GROOMED OR UNTRACKED SNOW TO MAKE TRACKS IN. YOU'LL KNOW WHAT KIND OF TURNS YOU'RE MAKING BY THE TRACK YOU LEAVE

You can improve your turning technique by applying edge pressure earlier in the turn and staying on your edge longer through the turn. You are probably applying edge pressure in your turns only when you are perpendicular to the fall line. You should now begin to pressure your edge just before you're perpendicular to the fall line. After you feel balanced doing that, try gradually pressuring your edge earlier in each turn until you are beginning to apply edge (and carve) as soon as your board starts to leave the fall line, and keep using your edge throughout the entire turn until your board is almost back in the fall line. Spend as much time as you can on the edge, carving. *If you are not traveling directly down the fall line, you should be riding your edge to some degree.*

Once you start to get the hang of carving your turns, try the following: As you traverse across the hill at the end of each turn, shift your weight to 75 percent over your back leg (fig. 84). This will help you maintain speed control. Concentrate on doing it until you finish each turn.

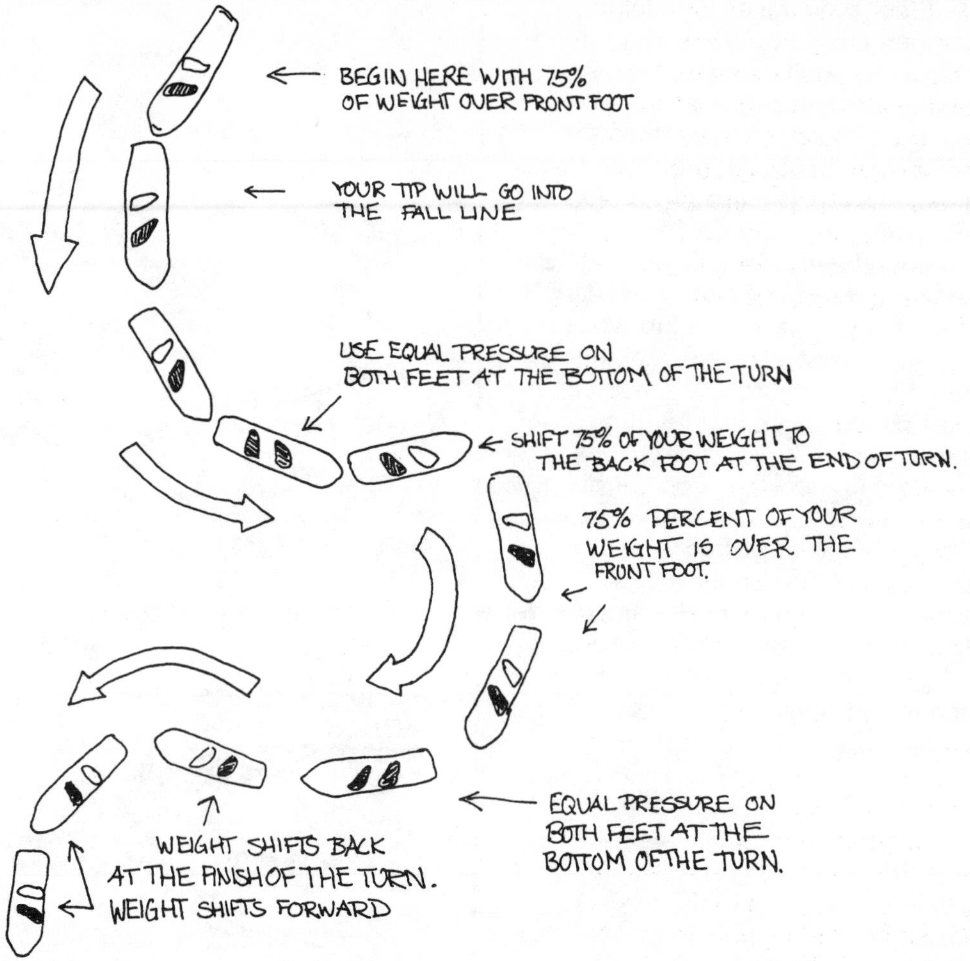

BEGIN HERE WITH 75% OF WEIGHT OVER FRONT FOOT

YOUR TIP WILL GO INTO THE FALL LINE

USE EQUAL PRESSURE ON BOTH FEET AT THE BOTTOM OF THE TURN

SHIFT 75% OF YOUR WEIGHT TO THE BACK FOOT AT THE END OF TURN.

75% PERCENT OF YOUR WEIGHT IS OVER THE FRONT FOOT.

EQUAL PRESSURE ON BOTH FEET AT THE BOTTOM OF THE TURN.

WEIGHT SHIFTS BACK AT THE FINISH OF THE TURN. WEIGHT SHIFTS FORWARD

FIG. 84: WEIGHT DISTRIBUTION IN A CARVED TURN

Now practice, practice, practice. When you're done, practice some more. Your goal is to carve with your edge all the way through the turn, except the brief period when the board is flat on the snow in the fall line. You must use all the skills you've learned—weight distribution, carving, flexing and extending—to make good carved turns. Get out there and make a zillion turns.

Remember to spend time settling into the turns. It's in this part of the turn that you control your speed by carving the finish of your turn. As you practice, experiment by combining and varying your maneuvers. Play with the timing and amount of edge pressure, weight shift and pivoting. Experience the results. What did you feel? What happened to your turn shape? Your speed? Your balance? Experiment with changes in tempo. Shorten your turn radius, then make it large again. What happened? Carve some turns on steeper terrain. Learn what to expect from your board, your terrain and your maneuvers. Spend plenty of time practicing and getting better before you go on to the next section. You'll need to be able to make good turns easily before you go on to the more advanced maneuvers on steeper terrain.

CHAPTER FIVE: ADVANCED TERRAIN, CONDITIONS AND COMPETITION

OKAY! YOU'VE MASTERED THE BEGINNER'S STUFF. NOW WHAT? ON TO MORE ADVANCED TERRAIN AND MAYBE SOME COMPETITION!

ADVANCED TERRAIN AND CONDITIONS:

Your next challenges are going to be riding powder, moguls and hard pack. If you're a pretty good rider now and can do all of the basic maneuvers on intermediate terrain, you're ready.

HARD PACK:

First, let's learn about hard pack. The most important thing to consider on hard pack is speed. When you move to steep hard pack, you'll find out that your velocity increases at an alarming rate. You can start off down the hill, and by the time you have made one or two turns, you can be going WWAAAAYYY too fast. This is commonly known as "out of control." It does not look or feel cool to ride out of control, and it can be dangerous. Keep your speed well under control on hard pack by making extra turns and stops and advancing to steeper terrain cautiously.

When you're practicing on hard pack, be particularly aware of traffic on the run above and below you. You are not the only one who may be having trouble controlling your speed! Make sure you have plenty of room to avoid other skiers and riders who are on the hill below you before you start. Ride defensively, and assume that people uphill from you will come careening down out of control right at you. If they look like they are out of control, let them pass and get a safe distance away before you start again. If you do pick up too much speed, stop! Pressure that edge, point your board uphill or, as a last resort to avoid a crash, use your emergency brake and sit down.

To ride on hardpack and ice, you'll need extremely sharp edges. The edges of your board have to be tuned (filed) so that when you pressure your edge, it can carve into the ice rather than just slip over it. If you are riding hard pack every day, then you should be sharpening your edges every day for maximum performance from your board.

If you fall on hard pack, you may not stop. The snow is so slick, combined with the pitch of the hill, that very often you will slide, gaining momentum until you get to the bottom or hit something. To keep yourself from going into a slide, roll over as soon as you hit the ground so that your board is below you (downhill) and you are sliding on your butt. With your board perpendicular to the fall line, carefully lower the heel edge of your board until it touches the snow. Gradually pressure the edge until it slows you down and you can come to a stop.

Okay, enough with the scary stuff. Let's get started. From up at the top of the run, you start by looking over the hard-packed run (fig. 87). The reason you look it over is to pick your path. The hardest pack will be in the center of the run, and there may even be icy spots (which will appear darker than the rest of the snowpack). This is because the majority of the traffic (which packs the snow) goes right down the center of the run. Now, look at the sides of the run. The snow is usually in better condition (softer, not as hard-packed or icy). There is less traffic (which means less packing) because the sides of the runs are intimidating for many people.

Plan your route to take advantage of the best snow. Try not to let the sides of the trail intimidate you. You can achieve the most control by carving your turns in good snow. Locate the icy spots and plan your turns so that you avoid them. If there are too many icy spots to completely avoid, you'll have to ride over them. Avoid any sudden pivoting or unweighting motion on the ice, or your board will slide out from under you. Keep your motion smooth, and be very aggressive about keeping your CM over your board and applying edge pressure.

After you've picked a route, start out carefully down the run. Make one big wide sweeping turn and stop. Then make another, and stop. Do this until you get the feel of how much speed you pick up in each turn and how much more dynamic you must be in carving your turns to stay in control of your board. You must exaggerate your motion (flex, extend, edge pressure) to control your speed.

FIG. 86: STEEPS AND HARDPACK CAN BE INTIMIDATING

A common mistake on hard pack is to forget to finish your turn. Making quick pivot direction changes to control your speed may seem like the right thing to do, when actually the slow, patient (count to five!) carve-at-the-bottom turn is where you will achieve maximum speed control.

Keep practicing until you can carve large linked turns down the hard pack, then go ahead and experiment with shortening your turn radius. You should be able to carve short or large radius turns down fairly steep hard-packed trails, keeping your overall speed on the run constant. If you are having trouble, review the section on carving, and try practicing on easier terrain. It takes a lot of practice to get good on hard pack, so get out there and keep making turns.

FIG. 87 : LOOK FOR GOOD SNOW AT THE SIDES OF HARDPACK RUNS

MOGULS:

Any strong intermediate rider can begin to learn mogul riding. However, your basic turning skills must be second nature because bumping demands total concentration. You will have to react instantly to make quick turns and plan your course as you go. You'll be in big trouble if you get in the bumps when you're still trying to figure out which edge to pressure or whether to flex or extend. If you're good at turning, let's go looking for some bumps!

Look for an easy bump run to introduce yourself to mogul riding. An intermediate slope which hasn't been groomed for a day or two is perfect. The ski tracks on the run will have begun to form small mounds of snow. Look for bumps that are small and spaced evenly, with plenty of room to maneuver between them.

Start by traversing the run, riding over as many bumps as you can. As you pass over the top of the bump, absorb it with your legs by superflexing. As you drop into the trough between bumps, extend. Exaggerate the motion to absorb each bump. Remember to maintain a correct stance in the bumps: shoulder pointing where you're going, CM over your board, head up and looking forward. Your movements will eventually be very quick, and a bad stance means you'll quickly lose your balance.

Make several traverses all the way across the mogul field in each direction until you feel comfortable absorbing bumps. Use your back hand to help lift and drop your stance (as discussed in the flex/extend section). This will help you absorb the bumps with your legs. Avoid breaking at the waist by keeping your back straight.

"Slow and go" is the next rule for bump riding. You may have seen mogul maniacs bashing through bumps at wild speeds, but you don't have to ride bumps in that style. You get to be elegant and gracefully slow. Steer with your back foot, and slide or skid your turns. As your skill improves you can begin to use your edges more. Make your turns wide at first, absorbing a few bumps and then pivot. Got it? Good! Next, work on traversing and absorbing fewer bumps between each turn.

Making a good bump run requires good planning. As you get the knack of threading your way through a bump run, always begin by looking over the run (fig. 90). Pick a path through the moguls as close to the fall line as possible, then plan the first two or three turns you will make. Then start out in slow motion. Make one turn and stop. Make another turn and stop. Use the go-stop, go-stop method until you get comfortable, then turn it into slow and go on each turn instead of completely stopping. As you gain confidence, you will find your speed increasing.

Zen and the Art of Snowboarding

Experiment with turning and stopping at various locations on the bump. You can use the tops as well as the sides and the troughs or gullies between them. Some riders turn everywhere on the bump, while others choose to turn primarily on the same spot. Practice them all to arrive at your best combination of places on the bump to turn.

A turn on top of the bump is the easiest to initiate. To demonstrate this, stop on the top of a bump and then look down at your board. The tip and tail are in the air. The center of your board is the only part that is touching the snow. This makes it a little hard to balance. But less surface contact also means less friction, which makes initiating your turn easier. To make a turn from the top of a mogul, start slowly down the hill and steer your board toward the top of the bump. As you hit the top, pivot with your legs flexed, then slide down the back (downhill side) of the mogul. Extend your legs as you approach the trough and direct your board back into the fall line, then go on to the next bump.

FLEX AT THE TOP OF THE BUMP

FALL LINE

REMEMBER TO KEEP YOUR WEIGHT FORWARD AND LOOK FOR THE NEXT BUMP

EXTEND AT THE BOTTOM (TROUGH) OF THE BUMP

FIG. 88: TRAVERSE THE MOGUL FIELD ABSORBING THE BUMPS WITH YOUR LEGS.

When you make turns down the sides of bumps or in the gullies, you can use the bumps to your advantage as points of braking. Practice braking on bumps by sideslipping down the back (downhill side) of a mogul into the trough. Use the next bump to help you to slow down or stop by skidding against its front (uphill side) with the edge of your board perpendicular to the fall line. Once you get the feel of bumping a bump to slow yourself, try it without the sideslip. Start off down the fall line and plan your turn so that you are in the finish phase (braking) as you hit the front of the next bump.

Another point to keep in mind is your stance. When you're in the bumps, initiate your turns with a little more forward weight than you use on groomed terrain. Avoid breaking at the waist! The reason for shifting your weight a little more forward is that when you finish your turns in the bumps, you will have a tendency to lean back, which will put weight on the tail of your board. This will cause your board either to shoot out in front of you or to go backward. Both scenarios will cause you to lose control, and ultimately you will fall. To stay in control, keep your back straight and your weight forward.

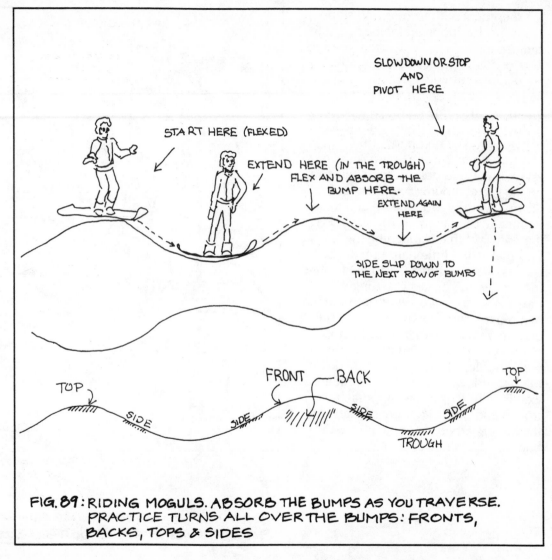

FIG. 89: RIDING MOGULS. ABSORB THE BUMPS AS YOU TRAVERSE. PRACTICE TURNS ALL OVER THE BUMPS: FRONTS, BACKS, TOPS & SIDES

Zen and the Art of Snowboarding

The keys to good bumping are practice and analyzing your experience. Make turns all over the moguls. There is no right or wrong place on a bump to turn. The ideal place to ride is along the fall line, initiating and making turns anywhere on the bump that you find convenient (or possible). Try variations with your turn radius, tempo, stance, weight shifts and edge pressure. Try skidding your turns and then carving with your edge. Practice first on small, well-spaced bumps, then as you gain confidence, gradually work your way up to bigger bumps on steeper terrain.

FIG. 90: PLAN YOUR BUMP RUN. PICK A PATH DOWN THE FALL LINE & KEEP YOUR ATTENTION ON THE IMMEDIATE TWO OR THREE BUMPS AHEAD

POWDER:

Riding in powder is the ultimate yahoo! The best part about learning to ride in power is that falling doesn't hurt. In fact, it's kind of fun. There's just a big poof of snow, followed by a gaggle of giggles as you dig your way out. It's a lot of fun to learn, and when you get good at it, it's even more fun. Riding powder is like floating—an almost weightless feeling of effortless turns.

When powder riding, instead of looking for easy terrain, you'll want steeper runs. That's because powder creates drag on the bottom of your board and slows you down. If the powder's deep and the run isn't steep, the powder will stop you. You'll have to experiment to find out if the run you select is steep enough to keep your momentum up.

Powder is a completely different snow condition than packed powder or hard pack, and you will have to use different techniques to turn in it. To learn powder riding, your first attempts should be in just a few inches, then gradually proceed to deeper powder. The main difference between riding powder and riding a packed run is that you don't use your edges for carving in powder. Instead, you will rely on your base more to glide over and through powder, and use your extension (unweight) with added emphasis to lift yourself up through the turn.

You want to float through the powder near the surface, not submarine underneath it. Start with some straight glides to get the feel of floating on powder. Float with it, don't try to force your way through it. Next, make some pivots. Use less edge pressure than you use on packed runs and more steering with your back foot. Point your lead shoulder where you want to go, and look ahead.

Unweighting is very important in making powder turns. It sets you up for your next turn and helps to float you up nearer the surface of the powder. You unweight during the extending motion of your legs. Lift yourself up and out of your turns using your back hand by raising it up as you extend your knees and ankles. If you have a skiing background, this lifting motion will be familiar, except that on skis, it's done by lifting the pole high before each pole plant.

SELF-RESCUE IN POWDER:

On occasion, when you're riding in deep powder, you'll dig the tip of your board in too deep and do a spectacular truncated swan dive into the snow, a maneuver which is commonly known as the "head plant" (see fig. 94).
When you find yourself in this position, it kind of feels like you've been buried alive. DON'T PANIC! You will waste too much energy floundering around. DO NOT ABANDON YOUR BOARD! You may think you can walk out, but believe me, in deep powder, at best you can breaststroke. Instead, stay buckled in and roll over to your stomach (a maneuver much easier said than done). Use a bunny hop (fig. 91) or frog-jump motion to maneuver yourself out of the deepest powder and into an area that is either packed or the powder is broken or shallow, then stand up.

Point your board down the fall line as you stand up, particularly if the powder is deep. It is difficult if not impossible to turn your board from a stopped standing position in deep powder. If your board is pointing down the fall line when you stand up, you can regain your momentum.

Zen and the Art of Snowboarding

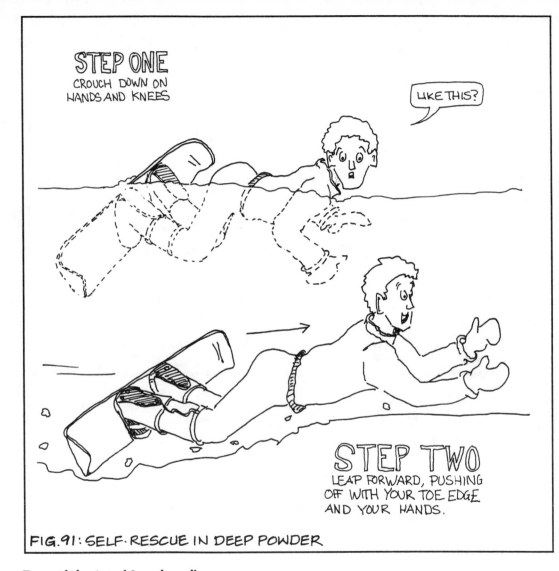

FIG.91: SELF·RESCUE IN DEEP POWDER

If you are riding powder in the trees, get a buddy and stick together! Study the terrain. If there are lots of trees, chances are you can't see more than several yards ahead. If you went out alone and got hurt, lost or broken-boarded, how would anyone know you were there? Maybe they'd find you in the spring! So go out with a buddy or a group, and stay in voice contact in forested areas. With a little common sense, powder riding is a blast. Get in it and set yourself free!

FIG.92: HAVE A BUDDY & STAY IN VOICE CONTACT WHEN RIDING POWDER IN THE TREES

ADVANCED MANEUVERS: (UNINTENDED):

As you are practicing maneuvers in advanced terrain and conditions, you will no doubt discover some new and exciting, although unintentional, acrobatics. Learn how and why they happen, and you will be able to keep those embarrassing moments to a minimum.

(HARD PACK) YARD SALE (fig. 93):

Here's a high-speed groomer boo-boo. Take any kind of fall you want, as long as it's on steep slick stuff and you're going fast. From the time you hit the ground to the time you get your board below you to stop yourself, you've probably rolled and slipped halfway down the trail, scattering equipment accessories and personal belongings all along the way. See, way up there . . . isn't that your hat? And waaaay up there, isn't that your brand new pair of sunglasses? Hey! It looks like a yard sale! You better start hiking uphill if you want to retrieve all your gear.

In order to avoid this exhausting and aggravating event, remember speed control. The faster you are going, especially on hard pack, the longer it will take you to stop yourself when you fall. Finish your turns! Be more dynamic with your motion and use your (well-sharpened) edges to carve. Be aware of

YOUR ITEMS ATTRACTIVELY DISPLAYED UPHILL (WAY UPHILL ON STEEPS) FROM YOUR POSITION

FIG. 93: THE YARD SALE

your CM; keep it (your weight) over your board. In the event you do fall, stop yourself quickly. Your butt will serve as a sled, so before you pick up too much speed, ootch yourself around so that your board is below you (down hill), and carefully dig your edge into the snow to slow and stop yourself.

THE HEAD PLANT (fig. 94):
This one happens in deep powder when you have too much weight over the tip of your board. The tip dives under the surface and takes you with it. Poof! You've got a mouth full of snow and probably will need to calm yourself down, then dig yourself out. Use the bunny hop (see fig. 91) to get out of the deep powder, then review your maneuvers (intended), particularly unweighting. Try to keep flowing with the powder; don't fight it. Keep your shoulder pointing where you want to go, and be sure your terrain is steep enough to give you the momentum you need.

FIG. 94: THE HEAD PLANT

MOGUL BOING-BOING (fig. 95):
This one starts with a "panic-turn" (too quick with too much weight on the back of your board). Then you freeze up and forget to flex your knees and ankles to absorb the bump. When you hit the top of the bump with your legs extended, YYIIIIEEEEeeeee! You've got air that you had absolutely no intention of catching. Since you're in the bumps, you are most likely on fairly steep terrain, which means you will probably be flying with some speed and for some distance. And, as they say, it's not the fall that hurts, it's the sudden stop. Say a few Hail Marys or whatever you might deem appropriate. Try to land such that it doesn't take a team of doctors weeks to identify all the parts. Good luck!

The most important thing to do to prevent mogul boing-boings is to absorb the bump by flexing your legs. Practice the exercise of traversing the bump run, flexing and absorbing each bump. Never lock your knees when you hit a bump unless you intend to catch air, because, believe me, you'll fly! Keep your speed and terrain at a level that you are comfortable with. That means small bumps at first, then gradually move to more challenging terrain.

FIG. 95: THE MOGUL BOING-BOING

Zen and the Art of Snowboarding

COMPETITION: SNOWBOARD RACING AND FREESTYLE:

Snowboard competition has come a long way since the first snurfing races in 1980. Back then, the winner was the racer who got the best running start before hopping on his board and crossing the finish line without falling off. But things have changed. Growing enthusiasm for the sport and modern technology in boards, bindings and boots have made snowboard racing a competitive and lucrative worldwide sport.

Today, snowboard racing is divided into professional and amateur ranks. Men, women, juniors and masters (over age 30) each have their own divisions. Races range anywhere from fun and casual local races to the more serious regionals, nationals and the most competitive race series—the world cup.

In any race series there is usually some combination of four different racing disciplines. The racing disciplines are very similar to those used in alpine skiing competitions. They are slalom, giant slalom, super G and downhill.

FIG. 96: SLALOM RACING: SHORT, VARYING TURNS AROUND 'RAPID' GATES THAT BEND WHEN HIT

RAPID HINGED GATE BENDS HERE

Slalom combines short, varying, rhythmic turns around and into flexible gates called rapid-hinged or breakaway gates (fig. 96), which are long poles stuck in the snow that lean over when hit by the racer.

Giant slalom (fig. 97) is usually a longer course than slalom, with longer, and wider turns. The gates are either bamboo or a combination of one rapid on the inside and a bamboo on the outside. The two poles are held together at the top with cloth. In GS racing, snowboarders (as skiers do) make rounder, smoother turns than in slalom to accommodate the speed and, to set up to go around gates, rather than hit them.

The idea of downhill racing is speed, which is also the key to winning. Downhill uses the maximum length of a race course with very few gates. The gates are spread far apart down the hill and not far apart across the fall line. This allows the racer to pick up speed by traveling almost straight down the fall line rather than reducing speed in successive turns.

Super G is a combination of giant slalom and downhill. The race course slope is longer than a giant slalom course, but shorter than a downhill course. The turns are longer than giant slalom but shorter than downhill racing turns.

GS. GATES HAVE ONE BAMBOO AND ONE RAPID. THE RACERS GO AROUND THE GATES

FIG. 97: GIANT SLALOM: TURNS ARE WIDER & LONGER THAN IN SLALOM

Snowboard racing is so similar to alpine ski racing that the races are often held on the same courses. The start at the top of the course has two posts which you use to push off. When leaving the starting gate, your leg will strike a wand which starts the timer. You run the gates as fast as you can by taking the most direct downhill course possible. You lose points for falling or missing gates. An electronic eye at the finish records your time as you cross the finish line.

If you want to learn how to race, you can start on a Nastar race course. Nastar courses are set up for public use, and you don't have to be a pro! They are for aspiring racers of all abilities. They are usually coin-operated. On a Nastar course you can learn all about racing technique and get lots of practice running gates. Ask your resort if they have Nastar courses and whether snowboards are allowed on them. Be sure to familiarize yourself with the rules and regulations of the course, and go for it!

FIG. 98: ASK BEFORE YOU RUN GATES

FREESTYLE COMPETITION: MOGUL AND HALFPIPE:

In addition to running gates, there are two other ways you can get involved in snowboard competition, collectively called freestyle, which includes mogul and halfpipe contests.

Mogul competition is very similar to mogul competition on skis. It is a judged contest, as well as being timed. The contests are usually held on steep "gnarly" terrain (pretty big bumps). The rider is judged on speed, style and technique. The judges will specifically be looking for tricks and aerial maneuvers, quick turns right down the fall line and runs that look smooth and totally controlled at breakneck speeds.

Pro-bumping is an exciting competition that requires dedicated training and endless hours of practice. But you don't have to actually compete to enjoy pro-bumping. It's one of the most thrilling spectator sports on the mountain, and the only requirement is that you be strong enough to either ride or hike to and from the bump course. Go on up and watch the pro bumpers. It's a lot of fun!

THE HALFPIPE:

The other freestyle event is called the halfpipe. The course and contest is very similar to halfpipe competition on a skateboard. The course consists of two high, round, snow walls on either side of a gently sloping floor. As the name implies, the course looks like a giant section of pipe which has been split in half. The walls can be up to 6 feet high or higher, depending on how much snow is available.

The object of halfpipe competition is to make a run going up and down the walls of the halfpipe doing as many tricks as possible, the more difficult the better. The judges will be looking for perfect control, speed, aerial maneuvers above the lip of the wall and tricks right on the lip and inside the pipe. A smooth style while performing amazing acrobatics and aerial maneuvers is what will win a high score. The rider will lose points if any part of the run looks out of control.

FIG. 99: HANDSTAND ON THE EDGE OF THE HALFPIPE

THE END ZEN:
So, you've finished the book. Did you learn a lot? If you can do all the basic maneuvers described, then yes, you've learned a whole lot. You may have even learned a few things you didn't expect about yourself and your new friends out there. Mundania is in your past. You've discovered snowboarding!

You are now ready to practice the art of snowboarding. When you're elegantly carving turns down that big one or floating through turns in chest-deep powder, your motion is effortless and graceful. It's pure joy and all yours. That's the art of snowboarding. May you practice it for years to come. Live long and ride strong!

APPENDIX ONE: WINTER WHEELS

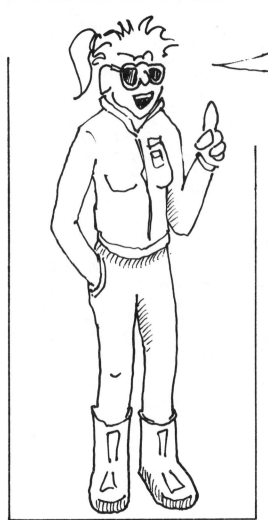

OKAY ALL YOU FLATLANDERS OUT THERE, IF YOU HAVE NEVER DRIVEN IN WINTER WEATHER, THERE ARE SOME THINGS YOU'LL WANT TO KNOW BEFORE YOUR FIRST SNOWBOARDING TRIP.

Yahoo! Road trip to the mountains! But before you take off, you're going to have to get your car winterized. Get your car ready before you leave home. Getting the work done may be difficult and more expensive out on the road between nowhere and somewhere. Whatever you drive, winterize it. Your mechanic can take care of winterizing your car, or if you are so inclined, you can do it yourself.

Fluid: In extremely cold weather, the water inside your engine freezes (and expands) and may crack your engine block. To prevent this, drain your radiator water and replace it with the correct antifreeze solution.

Snow chains: It is required in most states to carry tire chains in snow areas. They are steel link or cable chains. Beware of plastic "chains." In some areas they are not considered true chains. Call the state or highway patrol in the area you'll be visiting to find out what is required. You can either rent or buy chains. Make sure bungies are included in your chain set. These are giant rubber bands that will hold the chains snugly against your tires. Bungies help prevent the anxiety associated with hearing your loose chains clunk, rattle and chip the paint from your fender as you drive.

Make sure the chains fit your tires and that you know how to install them before you leave the driveway! Don't get caught belly-up in the slush with a flashlight in your mouth, fumbling with a chain hopelessly wrapped around your axle because the chain is too big or you installed it upside down. Learn your chain-up procedure before you get out there!

If you do have to install chains on your way up the mountain use the shoulder or designated chain-up lane. Drive 30 mph or less with chains on, and remove them as soon as conditions dictate. Do not drive long distances on dry pavement with chains on because tire damage may result and it will ruin your chains.

Mud and snow tires are much easier to deal with than chains, but in the real slippery stuff, chains are more effective. "M/S" must appear on the sidewall or it isn't the real thing. The tread pattern allows mud and snow to squish out the sides of the tread. They cost just slightly more than conventional tires and can be used all year round.

Heater: Make sure your heater and defroster are in good working order. If you drive a large vehicle or van or are planning to camp in your vehicle, you may want to consider installing an auxiliary heater.

Windshield: Get winter blades. These are heavy-duty windshield wiper blades designed to handle the thick freezy goosh. Fill your window washer reservoir with an antifreeze-type washing fluid.

Racks: You'll probably need racks to carry your gear on top of your car. They should be lockable and simple to operate even with gloves on. If they are ski racks, be sure they can accommodate your board. You can probably rent racks that will fit your car if you want, so check with a local shop.

Winter car kit: Even with a fully winterized car, emergencies can happen, so be prepared! Assemble a winter car kit and keep it in your car whenever you're driving in the high country. It should include:

Shovel
Snow chains
Traction mats or gravel (kitty litter works)
Tow chain
Jump cables
Ether-type starting fluid
Ice scraper
Extra fuses
Flashlight (with batteries)
Flares
Blanket or sleeping bag
Warm clothes
Gloves, hat and boots
Wooden platform for jack
First aid kit
Food
Tool kit
Sharp knife
Duct tape
Spare keys for everyone
Thermos full of hot drinks

The rental car: Make your reservations early and ask at the time of reservation for a winterized car with racks. When you pick up the car, have a board with you and make sure the racks will hold it securely. There's nothing quite like having your boards appear in your rear-view mirror, cartwheeling down the highway behind you.

Driving: If you are driving out of state, be aware of rules of the road which may be different from your state's. Ask. In some states if your car slides off the road, you get a ticket, go to court and pay a fine for improper mountain driving. Drinking and driving laws are strictly enforced in the high country, as they should be, and with out-of-state plates, they're watching you.

To prevent your car from skidding out of control on the road, never do anything suddenly, especially braking!! Drive as through you had an egg on your brake pedal. Leave extra braking room between you and the car ahead. It takes a lot longer to get your car stopped on a slippery road than on dry pavement.

It's best to simply avoid driving in bad weather all together! So call ahead for road conditions.

FIG.100: BE PREPARED, KNOW WHAT TO EXPECT

APPENDIX TWO: SAFETY AND SURVIVAL

ONE KEY TO HAVING A GOOD TIME WHEN YOU GO TO THE MOUNTAINS IS HAVING A SAFE TIME, AND WITH A FEW SIMPLE PRECAUTIONS AND SOME COMMON SENSE, A SAFE AND FUN TIME WILL BE YOURS

Life in the high country demands a bit of extra attention to stay safe, comfortable and happy. In the winter months the weather can be downright nasty, making travel and outdoor recreation potentially dangerous. But if you approach the mountain with information, respect and a bit of common sense, you'll stay out of trouble. Following are some of the things you may encounter, and some suggestions on how to deal with them.

BAD WEATHER: Weather conditions can change very quickly! It can be warm and sunny at the base day lodge and become a full-blown blizzard (colder than a witch's brass monkey) by the time you reach the top of the mountain. Always be prepared for changing conditions. Dress warmly and in layers. Always wear a hat, jacket or shell and gloves. If you get too warm, you can always strip down to your T-shirt, stuff extra gear into pockets and tie the whole shebang around your waist. You'll be hard-pressed though to figure out how to get your jacket and goggles to materialize at the top of the hill if it's snowing and blowing a wind-chill factor of minus ten when you get to the top.

FROSTBITE: Frostbite occurs on cold days, particularly if the wind is blowing. Exposed skin (nose and cheeks) and extremities (toes and fingers) are the most susceptible parts of your body to frostbite. First, the area will feel cold, then numb. On exposed skin, the area will look white. To avoid frostbite, ride with a buddy so you can check each other's face. If you get cold or have any numbness, go in and warm up. Never rub snow on frostbite! If you do get frostbite, go in immediately and ask for ski patrol assistance.

Zen and the Art of Snowboarding

FIG. 101: BE PREPARED FOR DRAMATIC WEATHER CHANGES

HYPOTHERMIA: Exposure to cold can cause the body core temperature to drop. The first symptom is shivering. In more severe cases there is confusion, loss of motor function, loss of consciousness and ultimately death.

To prevent hypothermia, dress warmly, with sturdy wind-, and water-resistant outer layers. Always wear gloves and take a hat with you out on the hill. Go in and have a hot, non-alcoholic drink if you're starting to feel cold.

SUNBURN: Ultraviolet rays at high altitude are more intense than at lower elevations. The snow reflects the sunlight, making the UV exposure even more intense. To prevent sunburn, wear sunscreen on all exposed skin and use lip balm with a sunscreen in it. To protect your eyes, invest in a good pair of shades that block UV rays.

RUNAWAY SKI: A runaway ski or snowboard is one of the most dangerous (and, luckily, rare) events on the mountain. Should you ever see one, yell out a warning, "RUNAWAY SKI!" and take cover. It's fast and it's sharp. If you can stop it safely by throwing an object in its path, do so, but remain behind cover. Big rocks, trees, buildings and snowcats are all good to duck behind. If you hear the warning from above, take cover and pass the warning, "RUNAWAY SKI!" as loud as you can. Even if you don't see it at first, take cover until you're sure it has stopped or passed.

BACK-COUNTRY RIDING: Beautiful, virgin powder runs abound in the back country, but before you go out there, you should be a strong rider. It's frustrating and exhausting and can be dangerous if you're not. Top physical conditioning is an absolute must. It can take most of the day making a strenuous hike to the top for 10 minutes of glory on the ride down. Go with an experienced local guide, and research winter back-country hiking and survival before you go out. Hiking and mountaineering shops will have literature and special equipment.

Guided trips into the back country are available near many major resort areas. You will ride to the summit via helicopter or snowcat. Although expensive, these trips are an excellent way to introduce yourself to the back country. The guides can provide expertise, as well as special equipment and fancy luncheons.

When going on a back-country excursion, make sure to get a list of required items from the guide company since you'll need more stuff than usual.

APPENDIX THREE: PERFORMANCE CHARACTERISTICS OF EQUIPMENT

WE'VE ALREADY DISCUSSED THE BASICS ABOUT SNOWBOARDING EQUIPMENT. BUT FOR THOSE OF YOU WHO WANT TO KNOW MORE, READ ON!

There are all kinds of advances continually going on in the design and construction of snowboarding equipment. To get the latest news (and hype), you'll have to consult magazines on the sport. However, for those of you who are interested, here's a general discussion on the performance characteristics of bindings and boards.

THE BINDINGS: There are two types, highback buckle and plate bindings. Either type of binding can be used on any snowboard. Snowboard bindings do not release intentionally like ski bindings do. Once you are secured to the board, it becomes an extension of your feet.

Highback bindings are made of plastic, and accommodate soft-shelled boots. There will be either two or more buckle-bale or ratchet type of adjustments over the toe and ankle area. Some also have a buckle strap at the lower shin. This system is designed to hold the boot securely to the board. The high back is for support of your calves and ankles when you're turning heel side. The advantage of using buckle bindings over plates is the freedom to move the foot and leg laterally for freestyle tricks. The softer boots worn with this type of system are more comfortable to walk and push around in than hard-shelled boots.

The plate type of binding is designed to accommodate hard-shelled boots. They are either metal or a rigid plastic plate running the length of the boot. There are two metal attachment bales, one at the toe and one at the heel. Plate bindings hold the boot securely to the board with no excessive play. The board becomes more responsive to quick and subtle movements of the foot when this high-performance system is used.

MODERN SNOWBOARDS: Let's talk construction of a snowboard first. Most snowboards built today use the many advances in technology from the ski industry. The snowboard will have an inner material or core, which can be made of wood laminates, aluminum honeycomb, torsion box construction, foam or combinations of these. The core is covered or wrapped with another material for strength and flex. This material is usually fiberglass, which can be mixed with kevlar and carbon fiber for other desired characteristics such as added stiffness, decreases in the overall weight of the board or increase in camber strength for rebounding. Some manufacturers put an aluminum backing plate between the core and the wrap for mounting the bindings.

The core is then sandwiched between the top and the base of the board, both of which are made of plastic. Embedded in the sides of the base are the steel edges, which can be either cracked or solid. The cracked edge looks like a piece of steel with tiny cracks in it every 1/4 to 1/2 inch along its length. The cracked edge construction gives the rider more carving and holding power on hard-packed and icy conditions.

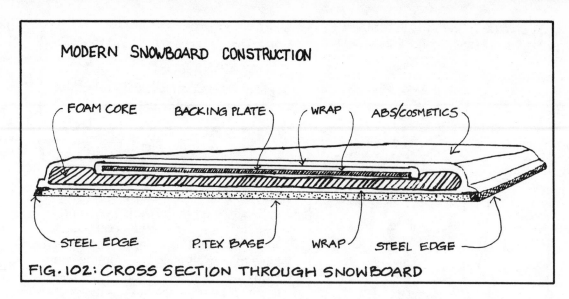

MODERN SNOWBOARD CONSTRUCTION

FOAM CORE   BACKING PLATE   WRAP   ABS/COSMETICS

STEEL EDGE   P.TEX BASE   WRAP   STEEL EDGE

FIG. 102: CROSS SECTION THROUGH SNOWBOARD

Okay, so now we know a little bit about the construction of a snowboard, but what about all those different sizes? The length of a snowboard is measured in centimeters with lengths ranging from about 130 to 200 cm. Your weight and ability determine the length of board you should ride. The heavier and more skilled riders use longer boards, while novices and lightweight people will use shorter boards. Your shop will have the latest length recommendations.

In addition to differences in board length, you've probably also noticed lots of different tip and tail shapes out there. In general, the rounded or kicked-up tail shapes are good for all-around riding or freestyle maneuvers, and the square or asymmetrical tails are for racing. The shapes of the tips can be pointed, rounded or blunt at the end. It doesn't matter that much what shape your tip is, as long as it is turned up to prevent your board from submarining in the snow.

Modern snowboards have sidecut. That means the midsection area will be narrower than the sections near the tip and tail of the board. The more sidecut a board has, the tighter its potential turning radius will be. Slalom racers, who need to execute tight turns, use a board with lots of sidecut. Downhill racers and freestylers, who make longer or fewer turns, use boards with less sidecut.

If you lay a snowboard on a flat surface, you will notice that there is an arc or curve from tip to tail; this causes the center of the board to rise up off the surface. This arc is called the camber of the board. Camber gives the board "life" or springiness. When pressure is applied to the cambered area (the center of the board), it flexes. When the pressure is released, the flexed board will spring back to its positive cambered shape. When the arc is reversed (pressured), the board carves a rounded turn.

Snowboards today are categorized according to the terrain and riders they serve. High-performance boards are made for those who compete or go all-out aggro when riding. Most manufacturers who sell race boards will describe the type of race their board is good for. If a board is termed a downhill, it's meant to go super fast and make few turns. A slalom board is made to carve short quick turns. Freestyle boards have rounded or turned-up tips and tails. They are easy to flex and good for learning on as well as all-around riding.

APPENDIX FOUR: BUYING AND RENTING EQUIPMENT

OKAY, NOW A QUICK DISCUSSION ON RENTING AND BUYING EQUIPMENT. YOU'LL PROBABLY END UP DOING BOTH SO HERE ARE A FEW HINTS TO HELP YOU ALONG.

You will probably rent equipment for your first snowboarding trip. How long you continue to rent instead of purchase equipment depends on how you feel about parting with several hundred dollars all at once. Renting is a relatively painless financial commitment, and most beginners start off this way.

Where can you rent snowboarding gear? Well you can start with a snowboard shop. If there isn't one in your area, try the local ski shop. Most larger ski shops carry snowboarding equipment. The advantages of renting in your hometown are that you don't have to bother with rental lines once you get to the resort, and you can select and reserve your gear early and be assured that the shop won't be out of your size boots or board when your big weekend comes along.

So, what if you live in the kumquat capital of America, and there is no ski shop for hundreds of miles? Well, then you will want to rent your equipment at or near the resort. And there are advantages to doing this: If you have gear problems, the rental and repair shop is right there so you can get free help when you need it. Also resort areas often have the most modern boards, boots and bindings available.

If you rent at the resort, try to select and reserve your equipment early. You will most likely encounter larger selections and smaller crowds if you rent from a shop that is not right at the main day lodge. There are usually several shops in ski resort towns.

Here are some guidelines to help you select the right rental equipment. First, let the shop know you are a beginner. They will recommend the equipment best suited to learning. Your boots should be comfortable, warm, snowboard-type boots with adequate ankle support. Your first board should be, when stood on its tail next to you, about chin or nose high. As you get better you can go to longer ones. It should be a flexible all-around fun board for learning. Make sure there is a leash, and make sure the shop checks the bindings for correct stance and fit with your boots.

To make sure you've got the right stuff, try it all on together. Flex your legs and ankles. Your heels should not lift more than 1/4 inch from the bottom of your boots. Your boots should not lift at all from your bindings. Nothing should hurt. None of the parts should be wiggly.

If you really like snowboarding and plan to do a lot of it, you should probably buy your own equipment. The best place to shop is in a specialty snowboard store. The salespeople there are usually snowboarders themselves and can give you up-to-the-minute advice on the latest equipment. Take their advice with a grain of salt though. Remember, you are probably a beginner or intermediate, and you don't need an expensive, top-of-the-line, racing super-pro hot-deluxe setup. A low- to medium-price-ranged all-around board will offer you tons of fun. Just make sure it's one that you can grow into, one that you'll still enjoy next year when you have improved a lot.

In selecting a snowboard shop, find one that offers a good demo selection. You'll never know if the board is right for you unless you demo it. You should be able to try out any type or length of board you are considering buying for a little more than the price of rental equipment. The shop should deduct all or most of your demo dollars from the price of the gear you buy from them.

Okay, you found a shop that offers demos; now you have to figure out what equipment you want to try. First, select your boots. (Most places don't demo boots.) They must be comfortable, warm and waterproof and offer adequate ankle support. Wear the same pair of boots when you demo different boards to avoid confusion in experiencing subtle differences in board design and length.

To figure out which boards to try out, first ask yourself, "What ability level and style do I have?" Be honest. "What kind of snowboarding will I be doing next year?" Armed with this information, the shop can direct you to the type of boards which are designed for your level.

Once you've narrowed it down to what type of board you want, you will select the length. You'll have to be honest again, not only about your ability but also about your weight. These are the two main considerations in selecting length. The shop will give you the recommended length range to try out.

Now take the type of board you want and try it in two or three different lengths. Then select another type of board, and try it out in two or three different lengths. And so on.

Don't forget about bindings when you are testing equipment. The shop should offer several styles to try out with your boards. Important binding considerations are adequate calf support (high back type), correct fit to your boot, comfort while turning and ease of operation. Remember, you will be wearing gloves and have to open and close your bindings every time you get on and off the lift.

Okay, you've picked out the boots, bindings and a board. Now just exactly how do you demo equipment anyway? First, take two or three runs to warm up. Next, pick out two or three trails that you are comfortable on. Make two or three consecutive runs on each trail with one board. Do several different maneuvers (fast, slow, big and small turns) on each run. Repeat the same group of maneuvers on each consecutive run.

Next, still on the same type of board, switch to a different length. Repeat everything. Make consecutive runs doing the same maneuvers, then switch trails and do the same maneuvers again. Now try another length in the same board and do it all over again. Once you know what that type board feels like, you can switch to another style of board. Go through the same procedure with each board.

Concentrate on how each board performs as you do each maneuver. Is it easy to turn? Does it seem to catch edges? Does it carve well? Does it feel right? After you've tried several different combinations you will discover that you perform best on a certain type and length. Consider this along with what kind of boarding level you'll progress to in the next season or two, and you should be close to a decision about the best board to buy.

APPENDIX FIVE: YOUR FIRST TRIP SNOWBOARDING

A WINTER TRIP CAN BE WONDERFUL OR MISERABLE DEPENDING ON WHETHER OR NOT YOU'RE PREPARED FOR IT. BE PREPARED! AND HAVE A WONDERFUL TIME!

Off to the high country for your first snowboarding adventure? Here's a checklist for the basics you'll want to have with you.

Snowboard
Hat
Scarf and neck gaitor
Warm ski jacket
Sweaters
Turtlenecks
Long johns
Snowboard pants
Socks
After-riding boots
Comfy shoes
Gloves
Sunglasses
Goggles
Bathing suit (hot tub costume)
Sunscreen
Chapstick
Screwdriver (adjuster)
Traveler's checks
Cash or promises
Credit cards
Driver's license
Proof of insurance card
Prescription medicines
Walkman, extra tapes and batteries
Emergency car kit (see page 108)

Don't forget anything. Call ahead for road conditions, then take off. When you get to the mountains, get local. Pick up a paper and find out about special events, sales, discounts, etc. If you don't want to be a conspicuous flatlander, blend in. Don't stare at celebrities, don't point and don't wear long-haired boots. Do: smile a lot, have a good time, wear jeans around town and meet some friendly natives. Take it easy your first day up in the mountains. You need a day or two to acclimatize to the altitude. Drink plenty of nonalcoholic liquids, get some sleep and don't eat anything too wild.

APPENDIX SIX: TROUBLESHOOTING

ARE YOU PERFECTING YOUR BUTT DROP OR SPINAL TAP? STOP!! ANALYZE!! VISUALIZE!! USE THIS SHORT GUIDE TO HELP YOU FIND OUT WHAT THE PROBLEM IS.

While you're learning to snowboard, you'll make plenty of mistakes. Following is a brief troubleshooting guide. Find the problem you're having on the list, and an explanation will be given. This may be sufficient to solve your problem. If it's not, refer back to the text where that particular maneuver or subject is discussed.

1. Falling over backward: You are leaning too far back or you have caught your heel edge. Review how to turn.

2. Falling over forward: You are leaning to far forward or have caught your toe edge. Review how to turn.

3. Falling over every time you try to learn a new maneuver: You are on terrain that is too steep. Learn new maneuvers on easy terrain, then go on to something steeper.

4. Falling over every time you get off the lift: You are not leaning forward enough or standing up at the right time or place. Review riding the chair lift.

5. Your feet hurt: Your boots or bindings are too tight. Loosen them. Or, your feet may be cold. Go in and warm them up. If they continue to hurt, have your boots checked for proper fit in the shop.

6. Hands and feet are always cold: Try wearing a hat! It will keep you warmer all over. Your boots or gloves may not be well enough insulated, or they may be wet inside. Try changing to dry socks and your spare pair of dry gloves. If your hands are still cold, you may want to try mittens instead of gloves, (they're warmer) or electric warming devices.

7. Unable to turn equally well on toe-side and heelside turns: You might be using the wrong stance. See section on selecting your stance. Or, you are probably on a double fall line. Find a slope with a single fall line.

8. Picking up too much speed: You are on too steep a run or you are not finishing your turns. Review the section on getting better.

Zen and the Art of Snowboarding

GLOSSARY

A

Adjuster, A household tool commonly known as the hammer; *see also:* persuader

Aggro, Aggressive

Air, To jump or fly on a board

Akja, A ski patrol sled

Alpine ski, Downhill ski

Avalanche, Snow slide, bad news

B

Back foot, The foot closest to the tail of the board

Backside turn, The same thing as a heelside turn

Bail, To leave, quit or give up; to change your mind halfway through a jump

Bale, Part of binding clip

Board, A ski or snowboard

Boing, To bounce off something; the sound one makes while bouncing off something

Boned out, When you hold your back leg straight during an aerial maneuver

Break, To bend

Bumps, Moguls

C

Carve, To use your edge to turn

CM, Snowboard lingo for center of mass

Cone, Short for conehead or nerd

Cornice, Overhang of snow

Crud, Undesirable snow, old crusty lumpy stuff

D

Dead, Description of worn-out board

Demo, To test a board or other equipment

Ding, A scratch or hole

Disk Lift, A type of ski lift

Dork, Nerd

Dog Pile, The pile which occurs when some dweebe falls getting off the lift and the successive lift departees have nowhere to go but on top of the fallen offender.

Dorkin', To act like a nerd, dork or dweebe

Down, Opposite of up

Dude, Male snowboarder

Dudette, Female rider

Dweebe, See nerd

E

Edge, Steel strips on the sides of your board for carving turns

Extend, To straighten your arms or legs

F

Face Plant, To firmly implant one's face in the snow, usually without such an intention.

Fakie, Riding the halfpipe wall tail first

Fall Line, The most direct way down any slope.

Flex, To bend

Front hand, The hand that is closest to the tip of the board

Frontside turn, Same as toeside turn

G

Gaitor, A cuff for keeping snow out of clothing

Garland, A turn made in one direction without crossing the fall line.

Geek, A nerd

Glide, To ride straight without using edges

Gnarly, Awesome, way good aggressive or difficult

Goofy foot, Right-foot forward stance

Groomer, A machine-textured trail or the machinery used to groom slopes

H

Hard pack, Snow that is slick, fast and hard

Heelside, To turn with heels on the uphill edge of your board

Hot, Great, the best or fast

L

Lead hand or foot, Appendage closest to the tip of your board

M

Moguls, Large bumps in the snow

N

Nerd, *See* cone, dork, dweebe

Nordic ski, Cross-country or three-pin ski

P

Pack, To slam hard; to help pack the snow using your body as a ram

Persuader, A hand tool, usually quite large, used to adjust gear, car parts, etc.

Pinhead, A polite term for Nordic skier (and you should hear the polite terms they have for us!)

Powd-air, Catching air on powder days

Powder, Fresh, heavenly untracked and unpacked snow

P-tex, A plastic base material used on skis and snowboards

R

Rad, Cool, good, radical

Raging, Going way fast

Rail, Side of the board

Regular foot, Left-foot forward stance

Run, A ski slope or trail

Runout, The flat area of a run beyond the slope.

S

Schlepp, To carry or transport objects, usually objects that are too heavy, over distances that are too far

Shred, To ride or tear up the slopes

Shredder, A way-cool snowboarder (like you)

Sidecut, The curve in the side of the board

Sideslip, To skid sideways down the hill

Skate, A propelling maneuver by which you glide the board over the snow by pushing with your back foot

Ski patrol, On-the-hill first aid and rescue team

Skid, To slide on the edge of the board

Slam, To hit the ground or an obstacle

Slide, To glide the board

Slip, To let the board move sideways

Slush, Wet, heavy melting snow

Snowcat, Machine used to groom runs

Snowmobile, Motorized one- or two-person sled

T

Tail, The back of the board

Thwonnng, The sound the board makes when you snag it on the side of a snow bank

Tip, The front of the board

Trail, A ski slope or run

Traverse, To travel across the slope as opposed to down the slope

Tweak, To twist or bend

Tweakability factor, The limits of flexibility or bendability

W

Wheels, Unusual or fancy shoes or boots

INDEX

ABOUT THE AUTHOR:

Elena Garcia, born and raised in San Luis Obispo, California, has been involved in alpine sports since 1968; first as an enthusiastic amateur, then as a member of the ski patrol, and finally as a professional instructor at Breckenridge, Colorado.

Elena has never been short of excitement in her life. She has worked for several years as an emergency room nurse. She indulges in high-gear hobbies, which have included exploring Mayan ruins in the Yucatan, scuba diving, surfing, and sailing a thirty-foot boat across the South Pacific.

More recently she has diverted some of her considerable energy to develop her artistic skills, becoming a successful water color artist and illustrator. Her work has been shown at various exhibits and galleries across the U.S.

Currently, Elena is residing in the San Francisco Bay Area, devoting her off-season time and talents to restoring and sailing vintage yachts, and painting.

ABOUT THE TECHNICAL ASSISTANT:

Kerri "Skeri" Hannon of Breckenridge, Colorado, is a former AAU diver, gymnast and stunt woman, who is now a professional snowboarder. She has written for *Transworld Snowboard* magazine and assisted in writing the instructional manual of snowboarding for PSIA (Professional Ski Instructors of America). She is currently racing for Team K2, adding to her already significant collection of trophies, including World Slalom Champ in '86 and '87, World Mogul Champion in '88 and two-time overall North American Champion in '87 and '88. In addition to her rigorous training and competition schedule, Kerri is ever present on the mountain scene around the nation, teaching, coaching summer snowboarding camps, organizing and teaching professional instructor clinics, and campaigning to get all ski areas to open their slopes to snowboarding.

Kerri Hannon: Catching Air

Elena Garcia: Learning

This book doesn't belong to you? No problem! You can order one for yourself, or two!

THE AMAZING, WORLD FAMOUS
ZEN AND THE ART OF SNOWBOARDING
ORDER FORM

Dear Amberco Press:

Yo! Gnarly dude. Like, I really consider this book (circle one) (a) way rad! (b) totally tubular (c) fairly cool (d) a total bummer. If I were the author, I'd (a) insist on my royalty checks in advance (b) sell motion-picture rights to MGM and retire in Colorado (c) sell world-wide distribution rights to Random House and retire to Colorado (d) sell my car and vacation in Colorado.

Anyhow, I'd like to order a number of copies of this book as circled: (a) five million (b) two million (c) six thousand (d) twenty (e) as filled in below.

So enclosed you will find a check or money order for $8.95 for each book like this one that I want plus $1.50 per order to cover shipping and handling. I'll make the check payable to AMBERCO Press and send it, along with this order form to AMBERCO Press, P.O Box 5038, Berkeley CA 94705.

Sincerely,

name _____

address _____

city _____

state, zip _____

(# books) _____ × $8.95 = _____

(shipping) = $1.50

(tax*) = _____

TOTAL = _____

* Because I live in the great state of California, I gladly include 54 cents per book that I order.